American
Indian
Crisis

American Indian Crisis

by George Pierre, Chief
Colville Confederated Tribes
of Washington

The Naylor Company
Book Publishers of the Southwest
San Antonio, Texas

FIRST EDITION, October, 1971

2nd Printing, April, 1972

Contents

America Haunted by History

My people, their imagination filled with the nobility of their origin, live and die in the midst of these dreams of pride. Far from desiring to change their habits of living close to nature, they love the out-of-doors life as the distinguishing mark of their race and repel every advance of civilization. You must accept and appreciate these truths before you can begin to respect and understand my people.

For those of you who seek to understand the American Indian, I express my views about my people and my country — the Indian country. For those of you who want to learn of and to help your Indian neighbors through understanding, I gently put this message to you. I do so that you and all American and Canadian citizens can get directly involved in Indian affairs. Once involved, you can use every opportunity to help the Indian people help themselves.

I do so without the slightest fear but that understanding will bring new hope to the Indian country and to my people — bringing them health, wealth, success, and happiness; provided they understand your intention to help and accept it.

To completely understand the American Indian, you must evaluate the impact that the tempo of history had, and, in many parts of the Indian country, still has on my people. For example, the white man has three thousand years of civilization to draw upon; whereas my people have less than two hundred. To get closer to home, my reservation, the Colville Indian Reservation in Washington state, was created by executive order in 1872. Little wonder, then, that the American Indian has difficulty coping with the changing times.

In August 1963, Chewing Blackbones, a Blackfoot Indian, died at the age of 106. This is remarkable in itself when the average life span of a reservation Indian is age forty-four. Forty years was the average life span in Europe when Columbus discovered America nearly five hundred years ago. How incredible!

When Chewing Blackbones lived to be a hundred, he had lived a long time. On his hundred and sixth birthday which occurred in 1963, he had lived a thousand years, in some respects ten thousand, and in some, a million. He had seen the world change as no man before him, even though Chewing Blackbones had been blind for his last twelve years. Within his lifetime, the world had advanced from the four-wheeled wagon of his birth — the wheel was used in Mesopotamia fifty centuries before — to the space capsule.

Chewing Blackbones was born in the world's most advanced culture, yet he rejected most of it. (I will give you the reasons why as we go along.) He spoke only his native Blackfoot; he was never hospitalized. When he was ailing and his family wanted to take him to the hospital, he simply said that it was old age and not even the white man can cure that. And then a smile would transform his ancient face and he would utter, "Maybe tomorrow I make a sweathouse." To my people the "sweathouse," a small, domed structure made of saplings and covered, was where one would pile red-hot stones in a small hole near the entrance, undress, crawl in, draw a robe over the entrance, and sprinkle cold water on the rocks. One would squat and sweat all the bad spirits from the body, emerge finally, and jump into an ice-cold mountain stream. Some old-timers bathed in this fashion year round every day. The sweat bath is big medicine in the Indian country — it cleanses the soul as well as the body. This practice, my people tell me, is as old as the Indian, which could be a million years.

In the beginning of the world of Chewing Blackbones, the culture was much like that of biblical times. Water was drawn from wells, clothing was homespun, candles and soap were homemade. Oil was used to light the lamps (as they do today in many of the dwellings on Indian reservations in Canada and the United States). Man's muscles moved most of his tools. Most men traveled by horse, as was the custom in ancient Egypt, or on foot, as practiced ten thousand years before.

Many wonderful things had come to pass in the lifetime of Chewing Blackbones. The steam engine made possible the transcontinental railroads. However, three thousand years before in Greece, men knew the principle of the steam engine. Yet before progress can be made in any age and with any people it takes human energy and the desire to get up and do for yourself. The Greeks spread civilization over the known world after the Macedonians conquered it. Yet today on the Tigris and Euphrates, men paddle hollowed-out logs or drift downstream in bowls of rawhide stretched on saplings. And from Baghdad, they walk back upstream for a thousand miles, just as the flatboat men in colonial times used to walk back from New Orleans to Pittsburgh.

3

The popular use of the printing press, the cotton gin, the telescope, the telegraph, the telephone, the radio, the automobile, the airplane, the television, and great advances in medical science — all of these wonderful things and many more were happening in one old Indian's life span.

Chewing Blackbones was less than ten when the Civil War began and ended and the American slaves were freed. The United States reaffirmed its pledge of freedom to include the Negro, but the Negro was never really accepted by the general population. However, in the final years of Chewing Blackbones, the Negro cried out against intolerance and discrimination which was heard around the world. In fact, the Negro threatens to destroy American society unless he is given the freedom, which in the final analysis is as much his as the general population's.

A strange thing happened in 1898. Americans went out of these United States to fight for the revolution in behalf of Cuba — against Spanish tyranny. Cuba was freed from Old World oppression, but our federal government took over. However, in similar fashion to the Negros, the Cubans were never accepted as equals by their champions. Even though they were given their independence, their hostility to Americans in the final years of Chewing Blackbones' life, gave rise to a tyranny that would have shamed the Spaniards of sixty years before.

The United States could have made Cuba a state in the Union (which would have precluded what finally happened); but the excuse was that it could not create states outside its natural boundaries. Yet it voted Alaska and Hawaii into the Union. The real reason that Cuba was not made a state was that the Cubans were nonwhite. The white man has repeatedly made this error (perhaps one must be nonwhite to fully understand); and he shall continue to falter until he realizes that every human being on this earth, whether he be red, yellow, brown, or black, is his equal. This is the shortcoming of all white men, not only

Americans. However, my concern is for my country and whatever happens to the white men here affects the future of this country; and this country is very dear to the American Indian.

Also in 1898, the Filipinos proclaimed their independence from Spain. But instead of supporting their cause, the United States fought a four-year war; then bought the Philippine Islands from Spain. However, at home the federal government was taking more and more of the Indians' land; creating reservations, then slicing a piece here and there in the name of public good.

While the record of the United States is not spotless, these actions were later repudiated. The Philippines were released. Since that time, America's attempts to support the cause of freedom in other lands have partially atoned for earlier sins. The federal government even set up an Indian Claims Commission to review all Indian claims and once and for all to pay its debts to the American Indian.

It is a paradox that the United States and Canada (freedom-loving as they are) should take it upon themselves to set aside a group of their own people and care for them as children. It seems that the federal government is looking at its wards through a one-way mirror. From its side you can see through the glass onto the American Indian, but from the mirror side my people can only see their reflection and say to themselves, "Yes, I am dark; I am different; I cannot help myself; please help me great white God."

The white gods never see their image, their weaknesses, their imperfections (you must see yourself before you can begin to understand yourself and those around you); but they look out over their wards and plan their lives. In this same fashion, the United States is looking out over the world. However, spending $2600 a year per Indian (when the Indian earns an average of $1500) is a pebble on the seashore compared to the government's gifts to foreign countries. But, like Rome, the United States will learn that white gods, too, can falter.

The Indian policy of the United States is fearfully like its foreign policy. Therefore, its support would be far more productive if it would do a better job of sowing the seed, instead of merely donating the fruit. Mind you this gift of fruit leaves the vines to wither and the branch to die, weakening and killing the tree ultimately. This is a sad thing, and Chewing Blackbones must have seen it in his older years; it must have saddened him deeply, because his country was very dear to him (the tree of life was the United States).

It is not too difficult to think of oneself as a god, if one is as strong, wealthy, healthy, and beautiful as gods would be if there were many. Some men in the past have fancied themselves as such. It is easy to fall prey to this notion; when the multitude have always shunned their responsibility and looked to others to care for them.

The pharaohs of Egypt, the Roman emperors, and the Japanese mikados believed themselves to be gods in human form. Until 1911, the Empress of China was a sacred being. The Tibetans still believe that God is incarnate in their Grand Lama. In 1776, continental Europeans, South and Central Americans, and most North Americans believed that their kings were God's appointed agents, ruling by divine right. As recently as World War I, most Europeans and all Asians took it for granted that anyone of royal blood was endowed with divine qualities.

Therefore, it behooves the United States to evaluate its policies, toward its minorities and toward foreign countries that it is trying to help, and bring them back in focus with reality. It must inform those they are trying to help that they will have to make do for themselves. They must come to realize that they, and they alone, can control their destinies, that they must ultimately help themselves.

Land, the Indians' Heritage

The United States and Canada are the first nations in the world who have set apart their native peoples on reservations. This condition created its own problems from the outset. For a people who, for the most part, were nomadic, to be restricted to a single place was a difficult adjustment. In some cases the Indians were moved great distances under the meanest conditions. They were moved from a place that had been home to them for untold generations to a place that in most cases no one else wanted. Little wonder this caused hardship and left the spirit broken. We must rekindle and rejuvenate this spirit. Can we do this? Yes, we can do this, and more.

Now I will tell you a little story of what happened to me in Autumn's bounty several years ago. I was returning to the Colville Indian Reservation, North Central Washington State, by way of the Okanogan Valley as the sun was rising — all nature seemed to cooperate, not only with the sunlit sky and the crisp, inspiring air, but with every tree and shrub arrayed in all the colors of rainbow beauty — the golden falling leaves of the cottonwood, the tall majestic strength of the ponderosa pine and tamarack.

I stopped to walk among the trees and on the fallen leaves to a mountain stream. I kneeled by the stream, cupping the cold water in my hand to drink. The water chilled my hand and filled my body with cold uneasiness.

As I contemplated myself, I heard, with a sudden, unaccountable loneliness there in the wilderness, the whisper of the wind in the morning reeds. I knew then, kneeling there by the chilled waters, that I had before me an immense journey. I knew then that I had to help my people in a direct and vigorous way. Therefore, I examined my conscience and earnestly evaluated Indian affairs in depth. I was astounded at the deplorable conditions that I found on reservations and the pathetic state of the American Indian.

American Indian health is substandard. The infant mortality rate among my people is twice that of the general population. Instances of tuberculosis among my people are nine times greater than among the general population. Incidence of death from tuberculosis is five times as great as the general population. Diseases which are largely controlled among the general population still cause widespread sickness and death among reservation Indians.

The poor health of my people stems from substandard housing, inadequate sanitary facilities, contaminated water, ignorance as to when and how to obtain professional care, and the uneven provision of medical services. In large degree this condition prevails among all impoverished rural folk in the nation, but my people suffer under the special handicap of generally living in remote and sparsely settled areas. In addition, more than fifty-nine percent are under

8

twenty-five years of age, as contrasted with only forty-two percent in the case of the total population.

Among certain tribes, illnesses due to microbes predominate; among others obesity, diabetes, and hypertension dominate. Malnutrition and respiratory infections make the young easy prey to flu and pneumonia. Most of these conditions take a particularly heavy toll among infants and children. Indian young people in their late teens commit suicide at a rate three times as great as other Americans.

Health and medical care for my people was an incidental part of early Indian education, even though funds were allocated for that purpose to resident missionaries. Army medical officers extended aid to sick Indians. Beginning with a treaty in 1836 with the Ottawa and Chippewa nations, in which they ceded some of their land to the United States, the goverment agreed to pay a specified amount each year for vaccines, medicines, and services of physicians while the Indians remained on their reservations. This example was followed in treaties with some other tribes. Underlying such provisions was the recognition that they were essential not only for the Indians' welfare, but also to prevent centers of contagious disease from menacing surrounding communities. The Washington government alone could act in the matter, since the states lacked jurisdiction on reservations.

By 1880 the Indian Service had provided four hospitals and seventy-seven physicians, and by 1900 the Bureau of Indian Affairs had made this phase of its work one of its major concerns. Later the Public Health Service supplied the top administrative officers, and the Bureau secured doctors, nurses, and additional personnel through the regular Civil Service. Then in 1955 the Public Health Service assumed the entire responsibility, and appropriations for the purpose have since increased. The Division of Indian Health of the Public Health Service are responsible for medical care, hospitalization, construction and maintenance of hospitals, water supplies and sanitary sewers, clinics and other such facilities for my people.

These functions of the United States Public Health Service, however, have not yet been closely enough coordinated with activities of the Bureau of Indian Affairs or with those of the tribes. This creates serious management problems, and results in the two services often working at cross purposes. For example, the Bureau is encouraging Indians to find employment outside the reservation. The Public Health Service in general restricts medical attention to those living on reservations. This means that a sick Indian, before he can become eligible, must give up a good job in the city in order to return to the reservation for free treatment, and after his discharge from a clinic or hospital, is afraid to leave this medical care. At the same time, it may prevent an unemployed Indian from seeking work off the reservation.

Indian housing is substandard. Ninety percent of the houses of my people have outdoor-rope wells (this was the practice in biblical times), or else water supplies must be hauled great distances. Practically all of our homes have outdoor toilet facilities. We are an outdoor people, but it is ridiculous to be outdoor minded to that extent.

Indian education is substandard. One third of all Indian children still attend Indian schools that are operated by the federal government; yet the education level remains far lower than the general population.

In 1952 (when this country was in the midst of the Korean conflict, and Puerto Rico became the first commonwealth of the country), the government undertook a national program to relocate in major cities of the west and midwest those Indians who were interested. Four years later, in 1956, Congress furnished special funds to provide Indians with transportation, tuition, health insurance, tools and supplies, plus subsistence for the trainee. However, one out of every three eventually found their way back to the reservation. Only thirteen thousand managed to stay on

10

the job. This program cost the government millions and millions of dollars a year.

Indian education should equip my people with training adequate to hold down a steady job. This is applicable to professional training also. They should be trained in tasks which will benefit the individual as well as the tribe. Especially where tribal scholarships and government grants are involved, the trainee should take a long look at his obligation to his tribe. A working draftsman should not be a graduate art major. A draftsman generally can get on-the-job training and be able to pay his own way, whereas a graduate art major must attend a four-year college course and be totally subsidized by grants and scholarships.

There are more than 200,000 Indian children of school age. In 1966, 16,000 were not attending school. Five school years is the average education level for Indian children under federal supervision. Their dropout rate is twice the national average. Many schoolhouses today are either dilapidated or lacking in modern facilities, so that much of the teacher's time is absorbed in activities other than teaching.

The Indian pupils come from environments ranging from the vastness of the Navajo desert to the grazing lands of the Sioux in the Dakotas to the swamps of Florida and the resort land of Palm Springs, California.

Some Indians today have professional degrees, hold good positions in government and industry. Others, with a meager education, live in grimy poverty, in communities where English is neither spoken nor liked, and often harbor resentments at what they consider past injustices.

Indian parents, without a tradition of formal education, find it hard to understand its needs or benefits. Poor families must sacrifice to keep their young ones in school. They have a hard time earning enough money for clothes and shoes and are loath to surrender the potential wage the children might earn. Such parents rarely give youngsters the incentive to attend school regularly or to continue to

11

higher levels. In such cases adult education, which benefits not only the parent but indirectly the child, is called for. Also, the community school, where both adults and children gather to see motion pictures, to learn methods of canning, and to engage in other activities, once was an important center for the group. In many places it has been abandoned; this is ill-advised. Such community schools should be more common.

Other Indian children come from English-speaking homes where there is an understanding of the ideals and customs of a technological society. These can find what they need in the instruction in public schools. But if the youngster does not understand or speak English or uses it only haltingly, and if his preschool education has been mainly in the ways of an alien culture, he faces serious handicaps.

Public schooling, unless adaptations are made, is not now prepared to deal with the nonacculturated non-English-speaking pupil. These children, unless they have had special instruction, are prevailingly overage for their classes and their work is below academic norms, the degree depending on their background and the type of training they have had. As a result, proportionately more Indian pupils than white ones drop out of school. Although definite statistics are lacking, it would appear that relatively few go on to college, and only a small percentage graduate. This condition would probably be ameliorated if more counseling were supplied at the college level. Every city has Indians who work in the professions and who, if asked, would gladly advise and counsel young Indians.

A child with cultural drawbacks seems unable to advance in school as he grows older. The need to learn an entirely new set of values which the public schools take for granted accounts in part for this.

On the other hand, to put a young child in a boarding school away from his parents may result in a lack of orientation in either the Indian or any other civilization. Even limited schooling may be preferable to the destruction of family and cultural ties and the resultant emotional and moral instability.

The Indian pupil's IQ is high, low, average, or not known. Available evidence supports the view that he has about the same mental equipment as other American children. Even the most gifted of either group may rank low in IQ tests under certain circumstances. These tests reflect "normal" exposure to books, English conversation, and even material gadgets, which underprivileged families, Indian or not, lack.

The present low levels of educational achievement among Indian children present a situation that will take time, even under the most favorable conditions, to correct.

One reassuring sign is the growing recognition among Indians of the need for schooling. Twenty-five tribes provide funds for scholarships. The Navajo Tribe has established a multimillion-dollar scholarship trust fund; the Jicarilla Apaches have set aside over a million dollars for the same purpose. The Southern Utes and the Ute Mountain Utes withhold a portion of their children's per capita payments, putting it in trusts which may be used for their instruction. Almost any tribe with money will make it available to its youngsters who are qualified for further education.

Unfortunately, many families lack tribal or other resources to give their young people training. Financial assistance to enable the child to remain in grade or high school, as well as in college, is often indispensable. These scholarships and loans should be adequate to supply promising children not only living accommodations and books, but also modest amounts of spending money.

By treaty, statute, and long, undisputed practice and policy, the United States has assumed obligations for the education of reservation Indians, and has for generations operated federal schools.

To fulfill this duty the United States appropriates funds

13

under two major statutes. Money is given to the Department of the Interior for the direct operation of its own Indian schools and also for payment under contracts to states and school districts, to contribute to the cost of instructing Indian pupils in public schools. These contracts are made under authority of the Johnson-O'Malley Act of April 16, 1934 (48 Stat. 596) which contemplates that the Secretary of Interior will fix minimum educational standards not less than the highest maintained by the state. This important requirement in the act permits the federal government to set and enforce standards and to see that teachers have a basic understanding of problems which develop from merging the two cultures. This money can also be used for training teachers in techniques necessary for dealing with children where English is used as a second language, or for engaging supplementary teachers.

The policy for years has been to have Indians attend public schools. Recently, however, Congress appropriated money to the Department of Health, Education, and Welfare, Office of Education, to be paid to school districts where federal activities have an impact (Public Laws 815 and 874). These enactments, however, prohibit direction or control over the personnel, curriculum, or program of the public schools. Consequently, when this money is used for the education of Indian children, the federal government is barred from setting standards or supplying the additional classes often needed by Indians.

Adult education was authorized by PL 959, passed in 1956. It has a fixed statutory limitation of $3,500,000 annually. To be eligible, an applicant must be a reservation Indian between the ages of eighteen and thirty-five, living on restricted or trust land. This excludes Indians who have settled in cities and elsewhere from the benefits of such training.

In order to obtain outstanding teachers, tribes with sufficient income could augment teachers' salaries in the fed-

14

eral schools, or hire additional teachers for children in the public schools. Even the poorer tribes might make a token payment toward their children's education, thus giving them an interest in schools.

Only if greater progress is made in the future than in the past, and if programs of education adequate for Indian children at each stage of their acculturation are developed and swiftly put into effect, can many of today's pupils be saved from becoming problem children, unable to cope with life. However, all Indian education, in whatever variety of school, must not preclude the parents' responsibility of preparing the child for a useful life. Therefore, the adult education programs must be concerned with the Indian of today — the adult, who in turn can assist us in educating and training the young people to be useful citizens.

Lack of development on Indian reservations is readily apparent. Even though the Colville Indian Reservation was created in 1872, there is no evidence of development. The government did install irrigation projects, however. After an expenditure of millions of dollars, some of these projects were never used; most of them are in disrepair now and are not in use. The cost of these projects are, in some cases, as high as ten times the land value upon which they were constructed.

The economic goals for my people should be the development of their land and human resources. The attainment of professional, managerial, and vocational skills should be comparable to those of their white neighbors. This will enable them to integrate with the non-Indian community on a basis of equality and not at the lowest income level. To reach these objectives, federal money and effort are essential. The longer the delay, the greater will be the cost in achieving the aims and the longer, too, will the large annual outlays of the Indian Bureau continue. My people need to be shown ways of making a living outside their reservations. Hence, new employment opportunities will have to be developed. This need was recognized in 1948 and a program to find outside employment for Indians on the Navajo and Hopi Reservations was started. Out of this grew the present Branch of Relocation, which assists Indians to find and adjust to work in new surroundings.

As a rule, the major value of steady work will be realized by those of the oncoming generation, who will live in stable homes, attend school regularly, and have the beneficial example of regular parental employment. Unless today's children have these advantages, they will find it difficult to break with their community's tradition of bare subsistence and all that this tradition implies.

In these respects the United States has a bounden duty if my people are to progress from their present poverty to a decent standard of living. On the one hand, they will require capital; on the other, vocational education for both youth and adults — and for all these services, a qualified planning staff and technical guidance for carrying out the programs. But no plan, however well-financed and expertly guided, will succeed unless its goals coincide with the values and aspirations of the tribesmen concerned, and command the support of a substantial number of them.

My people must be made aware that they have a responsibility for initiating programs for this purpose. Moreover, tribesmen equipped with the necessary skills should assume the responsibility for management and operaton of reservation projects.

Many reservations, however, lack sufficient land or other natural resources to provide an adequate economic base for their members. Between 1953 and 1957 this already inadequate land base was further jeopardized when the Department of the Interior removed trust restrictions from approximately 1,790,650 acres of individual trust-allotted tracts and conveyed fee simple titles to the owners. This opened the land to taxation and alienation. The chairman of the Committee on Interior and Insular Affairs of the Senate reported the situation as "alarming."

16

The desirability of removing the Indian lands from trust status should be approached realistically. This is particularly true where allotment dominates the use of a larger area, or is needed for the consolidation of holdings, or when it controls water or the access to nearby ground, or affects the economic use of other land.

Some reservations are too isolated to justify the establishment of industry. Even when this is not the case, the location of industrial plants on or near the reservation offers no complete solution to unemployment even though it may provide a higher standard of living for some. Yet, when the Indian attempts to leave the reservation, he is faced with the problem common in many parts of rural America. Namely, the difficulty of an untrained or semi-skilled worker finding a job in a highly technical society.

These facts indicate for my people a future both grim and complex. But its very complexity points to the need for help from many sources: from government, which bears the chief responsibility; from states; and from private groups sufficiently informed to act with knowledge and judgement.

It seems incredible, but the federal government did succeed in adding to its reservation problem. It added the so-called "heirship problem." In 1887, someone had the idea that the way to solve the Indian problem was to divide the Indian lands and give each Indian a plot of ground to farm. Overlooked, however, was the fact that most Indians were hunters, not farmers. That oversight has plagued the government ever since.

Indians were unable to make a living on the land. So the government had to continue its "trusteeship," manage the individual tract for the Indian by leasing it to somebody else, and give the Indian owner the tax-free income that resulted. The system worked fairly well for a while.

But, by now, the land has been handed down from generation to generation so that some small plots of 80 or

17

160 acres have literally hundreds of owners. The land cannot be sold because that would require the unanimous agreement of all the heirs, and many of them cannot be found.

So, regularly, the government mails tens of thousands of small checks (many for twenty-five cents or less) to all the known heirs. The cost of preparing and processing each check is often more than its face value.

Only Congress, by a special law, can put an end to this tangle. Meanwhile, the bureau hires more people, buys bigger and better computers — and each year there are more heirs, and more checks to mail.

It is clear at a glance that higher and higher spending by the government has not begun to solve the problems of the reservation Indians. The complex heirship problem is only one example. Many other things have been tried down through the years, but thousands of those on the reservations still live little better than their grandparents did.

The average income of my people is gravely substandard. An income of $1,500 a year is earned by the average reservation Indian; whereas, $6,000 a year is the average for the general population.

This, mind you, existed after over almost two hundred years of governmental wardship. After the expenditure of billions of dollars, the government was using the General Custer approach to Indian affairs: there was a total lack of understanding. In some cases, there was a lack of interest, and even resentment of and animosity for the American Indian, for whom they were paid to exercise the government's wardship.

You might ask me, "Are you against the Bureau of Indian Affairs?" No, not in principle, but in fact, if the bureau is going to continue its trial-and-error course across the face of the Indian country, then I would say in reply, "Why continue to waste our tax dollar?" Mind you, there is nobility in the basic idea of Indian affairs in this country; what I object to is the approach.

We must get men to head up this resurrection who are of reservation heritage, men who understand the Indian people and who have an appreciation for the land and the Indian country. My people are the only ones who can aptly measure their problems and resolve them for the general good of all; because every part of the Indian country is sacred to my people. Every hillside, every valley, every mountain and plain has been hallowed by some fond memory or some sad experience of my people. Even the rocks, which seem to lay stupid as they swelter in the sun along the silent riverbanks and lakeshores in solemn grandeur thrill with memories of past events connected with the lives of my people.

The very dust under our feet responds more lovingly to our footsteps than to the footsteps of non-Indians, because it is the ashes of our ancestors, and our bare feet are conscious of the sympathetic touch, for the soil is rich with the life of our kindred.

It is upon this ground, the ground of our forefathers, that we must build a strong house with building blocks of confidence, leadership, enthusiasm, understanding, genuineness, desire to improve ourselves, and faith.

The American Indian remains probably the least understood American of us all. To preclude further misunderstanding, and to ensure continuous understanding, we, the full citizenry of the United States, have a dual responsibility. We must help to restore the Indian's pride of origin and faith in himself. We must arouse in him a desire to share in the benefits of modern civilization.

To encourage pride in the Amerindic is not to turn back the clock. On the contrary, it is to recognize that government policy has hitherto failed to use this vital factor effectively as a force for assimilation and for enriching American culture.

Therefore, only men who have a foot in each way of life and an appreciation of both can effectively lessen the gap which divides the two and thus cross-fertilize both.

19

Harvey Davis, retired from the Coast Guard and a professional news photographer; Lawney Reyes, interior designer; Paul Wapato, electrical engineer; Edward G. Pierre, commercial pilot; Jeffrey B. Harrison, attorney; Carl Jackson, law enforcement; Billy Mills, Olympic gold medal winner; Dr. Fox; Dr. Perry; Wilbur Betts, engineer; and myself, to name only a few, are men of Indian heritage who went forth into the American way of life and achieved a full measure of success. We are the men who can serve as a bridge to enable others to move freely between the two worlds.

We can furnish a degree of understanding which will preclude trial and error. We are the men who stand on the horizon. We can greatly assist the white man to achieve a full understanding of our people. We feel that we have a responsibility and an obligation to our people, and we will discharge these duties with full understanding.

No one can give you understanding. If you don't have it, you cannot learn it. You have to be born with it; it is a birthright. If a person doesn't know this, you cannot tell him.

Of course this is not to say that in order to understand the Indian, you have to be a full-blood. I know white men who understand. A great many of the tribal attorneys are men who understand the American Indian.

The point that I make here is the point that I have tried to make for over twenty years. The point that I shall continue to make for twenty more years if need be, is that we have men of Indian heritage who are willing and able to help our people, but the powers that be do not utilize these good men.

I believe that we need some imagination in high places, the type of imagination that picked the United States up by the bootstraps a couple of hundred years ago and put America on the map.

Because of this, the United States was destined to accomplish great things, and as it evolved through nearly two centuries of changing times, conditions, and pressures;

20

our greatness as a nation readily became apparent. The expansion across the continent, the Civil War, the building of the railroads, industrial development, growing involvement in world affairs, the airplane, two world wars, space exploration — none of these could be foreseen by the founding fathers. However, without these trials — the plaques of merit and the stumbling blocks of ignorance — we would not have tasted the bitter fruits of fear and strife nor the sweet fruits of freedom. We would not have taken our freedom seriously, not only to cherish above all else but to share with others less fortunate than ourselves.

That is why we, today, are moving heaven and earth to guarantee, for ourselves and the peace-loving nations of the world, freedom. In order to achieve this, we are arming ourselves to an extent that heretofore was unknown to man in war or peace. It is our belief that we must be strong to ensure freedom.

The cause of freedom is not an idle pipe dream with us. Our nation was born under the star of freedom. And to a large extent, our inherent and undying love to be free, down through the years, made this nation under God truly great.

And my people, the American Indian, contributed mightily to that greatness. This country must not forget the contributions that my people gave, at times reluctantly, but mostly freely, gladly, and willingly.

We need to remember the contributions, spiritual as well as physical, our founding fathers found here in America and from which they borrowed so generously. We, and I'm speaking to my people, we need to remember and be proud. We need to regain that living faith in ourselves, the faith which carried us upright with our faces held skyward for untold centuries. We must shake off, we must lose this horrible shame which we have as a people. Sometimes in the past two hundred years we acquired a terrible inferiority complex, a living shame as a people. No one knows the exact time or the reason that this hideous spell befell upon my people. It might have happened when we were being pushed into the foothills of the Alleghenys, or when we were forced beyond the Alleghenys and across the Mississipi and the wide Missouri. It might have happened when we were beaten and forced onto reservations. And then again, it might have happened during the decade after decade of abject poverty. No one knows the exact reason we, as a people, possess this malignant shame.

However, take faith, my people, I know how we shall overcome this handicap. I know how we can take this negative experience and turn it around and change it into confidence, faith, and pride; change it into strength, freedom, and greatness.

The answers are simple and varied. The answers lay in our magnificent past. We must displace shame with pride, inferiority feelings with confidence, disbelief with faith and hope, weakness with strength, guilt with freedom, and backwardness with greatness.

We must examine the great contributions that we made to America. We must examine our history and understand it and use it to build a better future for us all.

When my people, the American Indian, controlled the balance of power, the settlers from Europe were forced to consider our views, and to deal with us by treaties and other mutual agreements freely arrived at. The pioneers found that in the southeast there had developed a high civilization with safeguards for ensuring the peace. A northern extension of that civilization, the League of the Iroquois, inspired Benjamin Franklin to copy it in planning the federation of states. Therefore my people, centuries before the coming of the white man, had found a strength in unity to preserve peace. Today we shall find strength in a rebirth of that kind of faith, hope, confidence, and freedom.

Only he who makes his people free, can make them strong; and only he who makes his people strong, can make them great.

By great people, I mean people like the giants who came

22

here in the beginning, our ancestors, whose conquest was the North American continent — and even more than that: they were conquerors of the western world — the land, the water, and the heavens above.

The Indians are a fine group of Americans, and don't let anybody tell you any different. As a people, their patriotism to country and to God is without parallel in this era of questionable loyalty. Not one Indian I know of is a communist or a leftist sympathizer; not one fascist; not a single one has defected or committed treasonable acts against his country.

The ancestors of these fine people, my people, on 12 October 1492, stood on the shores of the great land which was to become America and watched the first white man arrive. My forefathers loved their land then. Today, my people hold the same deep love of their land.

The continent of North America is very dear to the Indian — to us all. Every part of this land is sacred to my people.

By strong people, I mean strength in depth. I mean economic solidarity, planned economic development. I mean strong-willed men of courage. Brave men who have the courage of their conviction; who can develop their land, build their homes and mills from our vast timber resources. Strong men who can work the land and raise tremendous herds on our great land resources. Enterprising men who can uncover minerals from our untapped mineral resources.

By free people, I mean freedom to choose what you want. Freedom to do with what is yours as you wish. I mean that independent integrity that guarantees you the right to govern your own destinies. If you want your land and gold claims paid out in per capita, then your wish should be law. If you want state jurisdiction, you and you alone should decide this by popular ballot. Nobody in Ottawa or in Washington, D.C., should tell you what to do; rather, they should ask you, "Should we do this or that?"

The freedom of choice should be yours. We came before

23

the government and its agencies and bureaus. It is because of us that these agencies and bureaus owe their existence — without us they wouldn't be. However, in actuality, the opposite seems to be the case.

Indian: Who, Where and What

Life in the Indian country is very different than life in the rest of the United States and Canada. The way of my people is on the change now. It is changing rapidly — with legislators after our lands and special rights, with non-Indians waiting on the borders of our reservations ready to pounce on our virgin resources, and with the mixed bloods agitating, slandering, and causing rampant confusion among their own kind.

I will tell you of these differences and the effect that they have on my people who live in the United States and Canada. I will tell you about our history, our origins, the way we

25

live on the two hundred ninety reservations in the United States and the twenty-two hundred reservations in Canada. I will tell you about the jobs my people do, the government agencies that are charged with the responsibility for the welfare of my people. I will also tell you the reasons why we are different from our white neighbors, and the way we are accepted or not accepted by our white brothers.

My people, much like yourselves, vary from one another in appearance, in way of life, and in standards of living. Therefore, to understand us, you must understand yourselves. You must understand that a man is a human being. As a human being, he has the power of reason, the power of imagination, the ability to capitalize on the experiences of the past and the present as bearing on the problems of the future. He has the ability to change himself as well as his environment. He has the ability to progress and to keep on progressing.

However, we must remember that there are all types among my people, as there are all types among the white people. Some like city life. Some do not. There are some white folks who like to live in the country. They do not want to go any place in a hurry. A lot of us feel the same way, maybe even most of us. Therefore, many of us do not want to be enfranchised or to terminate federal supervision over our affairs.

Termination in the United States, like enfranchisement among my people in Canada, is a very bad word. The majority, eighty percent of our people, could not step up to be enfranchised; because they lack adequate education, the desire to leave the reservation, and other reasons rooted deep in the past. In the United States we have reached the point where we cannot talk about termination of federal supervision — not even to each other. We do not want to talk about it. If we do talk about it, we have rather harsh words on the subject.

Mind you, termination or enfranchisement by itself is

26

not necessarily such an achievment. Being terminated or enfranchised means renouncing Indian status with all the privileges and the restrictions that go with it. And an Indian takes a lot of convincing that this is a good thing. There are a lot of college graduates and professional people who are not enfranchised and who wish to leave their property under federal supervision. There are Indian professional people — doctors, nurses, teachers, ministers, and lawyers — British Columbia has an Indian member of the legislature. And Indians are working beside non-Indians at all levels, in stores and offices and on construction jobs. For the most part, they are sufficiently proud of their Indian blood not to become enfranchised. They also realize the advantages of development of their reservations under federal supervision. Therefore, success is not only to be found off the reservations. On reservations in Canada and the United States there are many successful ranchers, loggers, mill workers, orchadists, cannery owners and operators, arts and craft specialists, and many other enterprises.

It's a pity white folks have such funny ideas about us. Take Hiawatha now. He lived all right, in the fifteenth century, but he was not anything like the phony Indian in Longfellow's poetry. Then there are the murdering, treacherous savages of the history books. The Indian was not like that either. The movies give the wrong picture too: feathers, buckskin suits, and all that; like the Indians in the Calgary Stampede, Gallup, Pendleton, and other Indian days. A lot of the non-Indians really think that this is the way our ancestors dressed, but only the Plains Indians wore all those feathers, and the rest was copied from the Sioux and Blackfeet Indians in the United States.

As a matter of fact, there is no typical Indian, any more than there is a typical European. There are at least seven principal groups, who vary from each other as much as the Turks and the Portuguese. They have different habits, customs and entirely different languages. So it is difficult to say just what an Indian is.

Sometimes they look like movie Indians — you know — movies have these people, cowboy Indians. Sometimes you can tell them easily from other people. Sometimes they are dark skinned; sometimes they are white. And then the dark ones turn out to be whites and the white ones are Indians. Indians are as sensitive as the whites.

They are very sensitive. Now, some of the girls are very pretty, and, you seldom see them in sun dresses.

I asked a girl why this was, and she said, "They're too dark," she says, "They want to cover up." She said, "They feel they're too dark."

But you shouldn't generalize too much. The Indians of some tribes are darker than the others. And even in the same tribe you can find dark skins and fair skins living next door to each other. Maybe it depends on the amount of white blood. But that's not the only difference. Did you know we have eleven different languages across Canada? And a lot more in the United States. And those eleven langauges are split into fifty different dialects. In the United States there are hundreds of different languages and dialects.

Some Indians have almost lost the ability to speak their own language. Some use it in preference to English. Mostly the older generation cling to the tribal language, even if they do intersperse it with English.

It seems to be quite a common misconception that there is just one Indian language. And that the Indian tongue had very few words, and the grammar was mere gibberish. Anthropologists are constantly trying to straighten people out on this. Our languages have few words for abstract ideas, certainly, because they seldom needed them. But for the things around us we have every possible means of expressing ourselves, with a full vocabulary and a most complex grammar. We haven't the words in English to express some of our thoughts, and abstract ideas do pose a problem in the Indian tongues.

Legislation on Indian affairs was often enacted tribe by tribe or to meet a particular situation. Over the years there

28

has accumulated a plethora of 389 treaties, 5,000 statutes (many of which may have been repealed by implication), 2,000 federal court decisions, more than 500 attorney general opinions, numerous Interior Department and solicitor rulings, 141 tribal constitutions and 112 tribal charters, besides a mass of administrative regulations and a gigantic manual. This unwieldy body of prescriptions and directions has handicapped present-day management, with the result that many decisions are reached on a legalistic basis instead of on economic, welfare, or social considerations. And the delay and uncertainty caused by the need to consult this mountain of material have been frustrating to the Indians, the public, and the bureau employees, and costly to everybody.

Examples abound: Why continue statutes governing Indian agents when there have been none since 1908? Equally irrelevant are the minute specifications as to the appointment, compensation, annual and sick leaves of employees, housekeeping requirements, and purchasing details — laws which were adopted to curb the corruption in the Indian Service in the nineteenth century; the later Civil Service enactments and the public contracts and budget and accounting acts, which apply throughout the government, are sufficient. The statutes burdening the president with details of Indian affairs, such as discontinuing and consolidating Indian agencies, are other dead letters.

Though it may be colorful, it is useless to have present legislation prescribing how to pay for wagon transportation; prohibiting federal payments to bands of Indians at war with the United States or with the white citizens of any state or territory; authorizing money due to a tribe to be withheld if it holds any non-Indian captives until they have been surrendered to the lawful authorities of the United States.

A reduction of the repetitious reviews before decisions are reached will minimize paperwork, increase efficiency, and eliminate needless expense. Under present regulations, for example, technicians and lawyers having contracts with tribes must itemize the cost of each meal eaten while on tribal business, listing the tips separately, and must state the subject and cost of every long-distance telephone call. They then submit this voucher to the tribe, which sends it to the area office for approval, where, upon favorable action, it goes on to a field solicitor who, if he agrees, shunts it to the superintendent who, if he approves it, returns it to the tribe for payment. And, with all of this elaborate procedure, the amount involved may be not more than the expense of one telephone call or a trip involving a charge of less than twenty-five dollars.

The bureau for some years has been organized to delegate functions to field offices. This program needs reexamination to determine its adequacy. Is responsibility accompanied by sufficient power to allow the field officer to make decisions; is the authority placed at the administrative level where it will ensure the most satisfactory results?

At the present time there is considerable flexibility in administration. The BIA can, through agreements draw on skills in other sections of the government, and under the Johnson-O'Malley Act of 1934, as amended (48 Stat. 596), the Secretary of the Interior may make contracts with federal, state, and private agencies for the education, medical care, agricultural assistance, and social welfare of the Indians. The act is not broad enough, however, to allow the secretary to make contracts for the performance by outsiders of some services such as law enforcement.

Various proposals have been made to improve the administration of Indian affairs. Some of them are: abolish the BIA entirely and summarily, with no substitute; shift all the work to the Department of Health, Education and Welfare; spread it among other federal departments and bureaus; create an authority like TVA to fix policies to be executed by a general manager; transfer complete responsibility to the states. Sometimes this last plan is accompanied by a recommendation to compensate the state and its subdivisions for the cost; sometimes no recompense is suggested.

The simplest method, however, would seem to be to retain the existing setup, with the Bureau of Indian Affairs assuming somewhat altered responsibilities and functions. The bureau has the decided advantage of being already in this field; it needs only revision and redirection to accomplish the purposes which the present-day situation of the Indian demands.

To assist in areas where government personnel have been ineffective or have fallen short of the desired results, professional people of Indian heritage should be called upon to help. Many professional people, Indian and non-Indian, want to help the Indian cause, but are not approached. Indian affairs are the concern of all the citizens in Canada and the United States. Before any realistic program is abandoned or established, the entire citizenry should be considered. After all, the American Indian is also a citizen of the nation and the local community where he lives and he must not jeopardize his community or the welfare of his people or his fellow citizens.

The form of an organization is always important for accomplishing tasks undertaken. However, no organization pattern, however beautiful it looks on paper, will substitute for a skillful, understanding, courageous Secretary of the Interior and a Commissioner of Indian Affairs with competent personnel dedicated to showing Indians that they are the key to their own advancement, educationally, materially, socially, politically, and spiritually. They can use the key only if they take on responsibility perhaps a little ahead of what they conceive to be their own immediate abilities; and that that accomplishment, whether involving children in school or men and women in the world, constitutes a goal supremely worth their while.

The superintendent is the government representative on the reservation. Possibly he knows the Indian better than most outsiders. And yet, as the symbol of authority, perhaps he doesn't get as close to them as he might.

We have been using this word "Indian" a lot. Strange how a mistake made nearly five hundred years ago should still have its effects. When Columbus reached the New World, he thought he had landed on the outer islands of the East Indies, which were already well known to Europeans from the travels of Marco Polo. He writes of them in his journal as "Indians" almost from the beginning and it's too late to change it now. For most people, an Indian is one of the native inhabitants of the Americas rather than an immigrant.

Indians are increasing faster than any other ethnic group in Canada. The Indian population of Canada is over 185,000, and they add over three percent to their numbers every year. They make up one percent of the total population, so one in every hundred Canadians is an Indian, at present. Now, this does not include the Eskimos, who are technically Indians too, nor the metis — the people who are of mixed Indian and white descent who for various reasons are not legally classed as Indians. Of course, not all legal Indians are full blood. There is a great deal of white mixture in Eastern Canada, and this accounts to some extent for the differences in skin color and facial characteristics. On the Prairies, there are fewer half-breeds, except in Manitoba, where we have over 25,000 metis. On the west coast and in the northland of Canada the proportion of full-blooded Indians is higher. Most Indians who have no mixture of other blood are apt to have a coppery tinge to their skin, straight black hair, and high cheekbones. It is really rather difficult to know who, legally, is an Indian.

Many persons think of the term *Indian* as describing all persons of Indian blood. This is not the case. There are a great number of complicating situations and it is just not possible to provide a simple definition. Without going into all the details, however, I think it can be said that, under the Indian Act in Canada, only those descendants of the

32

original inhabitants, together with their wives and children, are entitled to be registered as Indians. There are exceptions to this, as the act also states who is not entitled to be registered as an Indian, such as those who have voluntarily given up their Indian status, or in the case of an Indian woman who has married a non-Indian.

The intermarriage between Indians and white has been going on ever since the white man first came. It seems to me there was more in the earlier days. You don't see too many mixed marriages on the reservations today. But it's not such a problem as you'd think.

There has been no difficulty on Canadian reservations with the acceptance of mixed marriages. However, Indian women lose their treaty status after marriage to a non-Indian. It has been accepted as a natural thing of no strange significance. There is one rather interesting legal situation that has developed, however. When an Indian woman marries a non-Indian, she is legally no longer an Indian. At the same time when the Indian man marries a white girl, the girl legally becomes an Indian. This gives us a situation where the Indian woman who was raised on the reservation and speaks the language fluently, is not an Indian, while the white wife, who was raised in a white community and does not speak the language, is legally an Indian.

In Canada, an Indian has certain privileges and some restrictions. He does not have to pay income tax on money earned on the reservation, nor does he have to pay municipal taxes. His property on the reservation cannot be seized for debt. He is given educational assistance, including university training, if he has the ability; and, in addition, health and welfare assistance is available to those in need. There are very few restrictions today. In some provinces, an Indian cannot yet vote in provincial elections; and in some provinces, he has not been granted full liquor privileges. There are also certain property restrictions. For example, he cannot sell his property on the reservation to a non-Indian.

The world is very different now than when the first trapper came here. We have progressed very far and very rapidly — but essentially man is still the same. He has to eat and drink to stay alive. He has to sleep to keep alive. He has to take a woman to have children. Yes, man is essentially the same. We are the same, but the world around us is different now. However, we ruled our world once and we can rule it again if we are willing to make the sacrifices needed. It is not an easy job — it will take long days of hard work and planning to develop our land economically. It will take long years of effort and study to advance our people educationally.

But we can do this and more. If we ask of ourselves the same high standards of courage and strength and sacrifice which we ask of our Lord and Him crucified. The populace thrust Him onto the tree of the cross and drove nails through His hands and His feet, and then, raising the cross, they allowed Him to die with anguish on this infamous gibbet. If we raised our heads and looked up at this example of man's highest glory, we might gain the faith and the desire to attain our goals. Let us go forward to lead our people, asking God's blessing and God's help.

We must pray and work hard and sacrifice, and through faith and desire we will achieve our goals. A soldier in battle prays like no man before (but he keeps a firm grip on his rifle and keeps a sharp lookout for his enemies when he moves forward to victory. We must follow that example and take up our cross and move forward.

However, some Indians don't try, and they don't want to work. That is the reason we need to understand my people in depth. Then we might be able to make him care — even inspire in him the desire to seek out the better life.

That is a point of view. And it's by no means uncommon. But is it right? Can you judge all Indians by those you see on skid row? There are far more non-Indians on skid row, remember. If an Indian isn't working, perhaps

34

it is because he doesn't need to work, because he has enough to live on for the present. Saving for the future was never part of the culture of a people who lived on the natural resources of the land. Or perhaps the government has been too paternal, and given too many handouts, and removed the need to be self-supporting. Or perhaps our concept of working for a living as necessary to our personal dignity may not be as near the mark as we think. Then again, how many Indians are sufficiently qualified to get jobs, when the unemployed non-Indians are lining up for work?

Generally, an Indian does not save his money. If he is making a lot of money, he will spend it. They think nothing of spending twenty dollars for a fifty-mile air ride to get their hair cut when half of them are barbers. So it is not a matter of how much. He is going to get the essential things that he needs to eat, and clothing, and then the rest he is just going to spend. They haven't learned yet, I guess, to have all of the things that we think we have to have. They are happy without them. However, if there's a reason to work, the Indian can work.

Of the twenty-two hundred reservations in Canada, very few of them are near towns. So if you've got a house and some land on the reservation, how do you get a job? You do what you can on the reservation — farm, maybe. There are plenty of white men unemployed. There is a lot to be said for living on the reservation. However, a lot of white people think the reservation is some sort of concentration camp. But we've got our own land, our own way of life. There is no harm in living on reservations, as long as we can develop our lands and take care of our own.

Many Indians are quite satisfied with living on reservations. They don't look for mansions or anything like that. There are a few improvements that they feel they have to have. Generally city life doesn't agree with them. They don't care for the city. Even if they have to stay in the city two days it bothers them. They are just not used to it. When you're born on the farm, you definitely want to stay with the farm. You can take the man away from the country, but you can't always get the country out of the man.

You've met non-Indians who feel the same way. This isn't necessarily an Indian characteristic — though most of the Indians live in the country, and most of them feel this way. They're people of nature. Talk to an Indian who lives off the reservation, in the city, and chances are he longs to get back home.

I don't care how long an Indian goes away from his reservation. They live in the city; they always go back. They were born on the reservation and they love the place and would like to see their friends and relatives.

There are all kinds of Indians with all kinds of ideas. However, mostly my people are different from the white man in subtle, spiritual ways.

Generally, the Indians are wonderful people. My people are probably the most loyal people that I know. Once they are your friends, they'll do anything for you. You have to prove yourself to them. It takes quite a little while. They have to be sure that you're sincere and, when they are, you can do most anything and they'll go along with you. An Indian is a really great guy — you get to know him, work with him, be around him — I think they're very honest. Basically they're honest until they're corrupted by the non-Indians.

This may surprise people who see the Indians as something so very different and very dramatic. But actually, these people are the greatest conformists that you can find. They like to keep together, and particularly on the reservations, and anyone who shows any particular initiative in the way of getting a better education, of improving his lot so that he stands out above the others on the reservation, is often looked down upon.

Sometimes we wonder if we're looked down on by the white people too. Maybe we don't dress the same. Out in the country we dress like country folks, jeans, old clothes,

36

etc. The Indians who work in the city dress like the rest of the city folks. Up north you'll find Indians dressed for the cold weather, like Eskimos.

One of the subjects we haven't mentioned is the Indians' names. They vary in different parts of the country. In the west they're mostly taken from the missionaries and the early traders. Names like Kelly, and Johnson and McDonald. In the plains they're mostly English translations of the original Indian names — beautiful, colorful names for the most part: Starlight, Eagletail, Heavenfire, Coming Daylight, Wandering Spirit. Some names are descriptive of their ancestors, like Big Belly, Many Wounds, Born with a Tooth and Pretty Young Man. There are names from nature: Sweet Grass, Red Bird, Big Swan, Grasshopper, or Standing at the Door, Shot on Both Sides, Mistaken Chief, and Standing Alone. In the east the names are of many kinds — the original untranslated Indian, like *Wooteny* or *Wabush,* well mixed in with English sounding names. In Quebec there are French names — and they speak French too. And in the Maritimes they're very similar to the West Coast. Some of the names sound very funny to us when they're not understood. Stinking Saddle Blanket is in reality an honorary title, meaning that he was so constantly on the warpath that he didn't even have time to air his saddle blanket.

I've known people who have taken part of their name, which has an English sound to it, and retained this name. Such as Many Grey Horses. This name was changed to Grey. Or, A Young Man — this was changed to Young. There is one story told about a woman on the Blackfoot reservation named Mrs. Studhorse, who was considering changing her name, and, when asking for advice on a good name that she could use, someone suggested the name of Mrs. Don't Like Horses.

What is an Indian? Apparently he is like all other citizens in Canada and the United States and yet he is different.

Different in a very special way. He is a product of his history, his culture, his problems, his likes, and dislikes.

Termination:
A Bad Word for
Bad Deeds

House Concurrent Resolution 108,[1] adopted in 1953, sent the word *termination* spreading like a prairie fire or a pestilence through the Indian country. It stirred conflicting reactions among my people; to some it meant the severing of ties already loose and ineffective; others welcomed it as a promise of early sharing in the tribal patrimony. Many outsiders realized that it provided a first step towards acquiring Indian resources. The great majority of my people, however, feared the consequences. The action of Congress, accompanied by the phrase "as rapidly as possible," sounded to them like the stroke of doom.

Resolution 108 was cast in terms granting my people

their rights and prerogatives as American citizens. Its stated purpose was to free them from federal controls and supervision, end their wardship, and make them subject to the same laws and entitled to the same privileges as other citizens.

However, my people were already citizens by federal law; they had all the rights possessed by their white neighbors. The term *wards,* applied to them, was, and had for a long time been, misleading. Except for the federal prohibitions against selling alcoholic beverages to Indians, repealed in 1953, they were subject to no greater federal control of their persons than any other citizens; they paid state and federal taxes the same as white people, unless specifically exempted by treaty agreement or statute. Most of the exemptions applied only to real estate or income from trust property. The property the government held in trust for them was supervised as in any other trust, although some claimed that the government's management was not effective. The restrictions and the trusts, however, had not been imposed by the government but, by and large, had resulted from covenants made by my people with the United States in the form of treaties, agreements, statutes, and policies designed to protect them from losing their land and to assure the right of self-government, the inalienability and immunity from taxes of their land, and the services which the United States provided.

Termination is not a new goal; but the word itself has remained a loose one without definite meaning. It may signify any one or all of the following:

A relaxation of unnecessary federal supervision over the government and business of Indian tribes, and less control over the leasing and use of trust allotments of individuals.

The rapid destruction of a tribal government that has operated for generations, thereby uprooting complex federal, tribal, and state relationships which are defined in hundreds of treaties, statutes, and court decisions.

The forced sale of a substantial part of tribal land and the dissolution of the trust on all allotments of members of terminated tribes.

The subjecting of all tribal and trust-allotted land to state taxation regardless of the ability of the Indians to pay.

The applying of general state criminal and civil laws to Indians in place of federal and tribal laws suited to their special needs.

The abandonment by the United States of education, medical and hospital treatment, road building, and other functions, and of technical and administrative services and guidance to Indians in the management of their own affairs, without giving any assurance that the necessary services will be available from other sources as they are to other citizens.

A violation of the expressed or implied obligations of treaties and agreements between the United States and a tribe for exemption from taxation, self-government, and performance of federal services without these changes having had the unqualified consent of the tribe.

The termination laws enacted since 1954 produced, or were capable of effecting, all of these consequences.

Basically, the government had undertaken obligations and ensured benefits affecting all the tribes under the treaty and commerce clauses of the Constitution. The complex tribal relations with the United States, with the states in which the reservations lay, as well as with adjacent communities and other tribes, were, all of them, dependent upon the permanence of what the United States had guaranteed. Even legal specialists can have no full compre-

41

hension of the tangle of readjustments involved in the concept of termination. Neither they nor the tribes can foresee what measures will be required to make sure that obligations now resting on the United States will somehow be fulfilled. What my people fear, therefore, is a transitional period (not the first they have experienced) in which treaties will be breached and solemn agreements ignored; their land, tribal and allotted, lost; and necessary public services furnished by the United States withdrawn, without being replaced by others from the states.

Repeatedly in the past, congressional action in such matters has cost the United States large sums in the later settling of claims or in defending lawsuits. Error or oversight in the termination today may tomorrow call for the payment of unanticipated indemnities.

The Indian whose interest does not coincide with termination, whether or not he senses the difficulties, would usually not willingly substitute for government by his tribe a control by an individual state, one which would subject him and his community to unfamiliar civil and criminal laws frequently enforced in tribunals where impartial justice has not been given because of discrimination, lack of understanding or sympathy. He could not be sure that the state would recognize the existing obligations of the United States or provide equal services. And, in any case, state legislators could not be expected to fit their legal system into the customs and hopes of my people, who form a minority of the citizenry.

Since Resolution 108 was adopted by Congress, eleven basic termination laws have been passed to implement it. While the six termination laws enacted in 1954 emphasized their purpose of ending federal supervision over Indian property and terminating the services furnished Indians by the United States because they are Indians, they, in fact, abolished the home rule governments of the Klamath, Menominee, Paiute and other tribes; forced the sale of large amounts of land, including forest areas, of the Klamath Tribe; and made both tribal and allotted trust land taxable by the states.

Since 1950 the major controversy in Indian affairs has been whether the United States should follow a program of pressing for prompt termination of tribes without the consent of their members. This appeared to be the goal until September, 1958, when Secretary of the Interior, Fred A. Seaton, in a radio broadcast in Flagstaff, Arizona, stated that none would be terminated without the consent of its members.

From the date of Seaton's speech until 1961, confusion has existed, the secretary seeming to espouse one policy, and the Bureau of Indian Affairs another. All the time, moreover, Joint Resolution 108, stating the policy of Congress, has been in effect.

Termination aroused protests from my people, state legislators, and interested citizens. The number and vigor of the outcries and the difficulties encountered in trying to put the enactments into effect somewhat cooled the ardor of the terminationists. Though the full consequences of these measures cannot yet be estimated, it became evident that termination, instead of being a simple process, entails countless problems. The upheaval among the Indians would be not unlike that caused by superimposing the laws of New York on New Mexico with its different needs, people, cultural and legal heritage.

What alarmed the tribesmen also threatened many whites with financial losses. Notable examples are the stores of the Menominee forest in Wisconsin and the Klamath forest in southern Oregon.

The Menominee Act jeopardized the continued existence of the tribal forest, one of the last unspoiled timber areas of the northern midwest. Wisconsin, recognizing the importance of keeping this resource intact so that it could yield perpetually, took measures to acquire it for the state in the event of a sale.

The Klamath forest, containing approximately 590,000 acres of tribally owned commercial timberland, the finest stand of Ponderosa pine in the West, is located in southern Oregon. Under the management of the Indian service, the annual cut was limited, looking to sustaining the yield of the forest permanently. The forest on the Klamath Indian reservation supplies raw material to the principal industries of the Klamath basin.

When the program prescribed under the original termination act was studied, it was realized that carrying it out would not only be disastrous to the interests of my people, but gravely injurious to the economy of the whole region.

The management specialists apppointed by the federal government estimated, in 1956, that the act would require the sale of almost three billion feet of saw timber in a period of one year, within an economic area in which the sawmill production was 350 million feet a year.

To throw so large a volume on the market all at once would have resulted in a forced disposal. Bidding would have had to be on a wholesale basis, at figures far below those being realized on current sales of small lots of timber. The buyers would be tempted to hurry the cut of their timber and market it as rapidly as possible to recoup their investment and save on interest and taxes. The resulted flooding of lumber on the market would depress prices for other producers and lower the revenues to the government from the sale of timber on its nearby national forest lands by approximately fifty million dollars. When this large acreage was denuded of its growth, lumber mills would be short of logs, the community would suffer from loss of employment and the profits of forest products. The buyers, under very limited state reforestation restrictions, could abandon the cutover lands, exposing them to damaging erosion and impairing the watershed. Realization of these factors aroused community and industry leaders, conservationists, and my people to demand amendments to the law which would protect the financial interest of the Indians and safeguard the economic well-being of the area.

The act had to be changed in a number of ways. One amendment required the tribal timber to be divided into units and offered for sale only to buyers who would agree (on penalty of forfeiting the purchase) to manage the forest according to sustained yield procedures so as to furnish a continuing supply of timber and conserve water, soil, and trees.

On those conditions only one of the eleven units offered has been obtained by a private buyer. The other ten units, under the altered law, were acquired by the United States on April 1, 1961, at the cost of nearly $69 million. This same amendment provided that the United States also had to take over the Klamath marsh in order to preserve it as a vital part of the migratory bird flyway and a source of the Williamson River. The cost of the marsh was $476,000.

The consequences of the Klamath Termination Act had obviously not been adequately weighed either by the Department of the Interior or by Congress; hence four successive changes in the basic measure proved necessary.

The law and its amendments, taken together, furnish an example (not the only one in Indian history) of ill-considered and unsuccessful attempts to deal (in an all-inclusive measure) with Indians irrespective of their special way of life, their location, and property holdings. It also demonstrates that no termination of tribes, especially those with large properties, should ever be deemed merely an Indian problem. It is inevitably a national problem, one upon the solution of which depends the welfare of people both near and far.

In still another sense termination offers no pat answer to "the Indian problem," for my people remain. They remain (in a culture much like that of ancient Egypt) mostly where they were and as they were. For the government to act out of a sense of frustration and of haste to rid itself of the vexing questions involved in administering Indian affairs is bound to ensure failure. American Indian policy, if it is to succeed, must aim at helping Indians to help themselves in whatever is their prevailing social and economic framework. As this is accomplished, politicians must cease to speak with forked tongue. To get the full cooperation of my people, the Congress should resend House Concurrent Resolution 108, and then pass a resolution for all time precluding termination and other policies which break faith with my people.

However, my people must bear in mind that no government can support its people, for the simple reason that a government must derive its support from the people. The general population would do well to remember this too.

---

1 HOUSE CONCURRENT RESOLUTION, 83RD CONGRESS, 1ST SESSION, August 1, 1953

Whereas it is the policy of Congress, as rapidly as possible, to make the Indians within the territorial limits of the United States subject to the same laws and entitled to the same privileges and responsibilities as are applicable to other citizens of the United States, to end their status as wards of the United States, and to grant them all of the rights and prerogatives pertaining to American citizenship; and
Whereas the Indians within the territorial limits of the United States should assume their full responsibilities as American citizens: Now, therefore, be it
Resolved by the House of Representatives (the Senate concurring), That it is declared to be the sense of Congress that, at the earliest possible time, all of the Indian tribes and the individual members thereof located within the States of California, Florida, New York, and Texas; and all of the following named Indian tribes and individual members thereof, should be free from federal supervision and control and from all disabilities and limitations specially applicable to Indians: The Flathead Tribe of Montana, The Klamath Tribe of Oregon, the Menominee Tribe of Wisconsin, the Potowatamie Tribe of Kansas and Nebraska, and those members of the Chippewa Tribe who are on the Turtle Mountain Reservation, North Dakota. It is further declared to be the sense of Congress that, upon the release of such tribes and individual members thereof from such disabilities and limitations, all offices of the Bureau of Indian Affairs in the States of California, Florida, New York, and Texas and all other offices of the Bureau of Indian Affairs whose primary purpose was to serve any Indian tribe or individual Indian freed from Federal supervision should be abolished. It is further declared to be the sense of Congress that the Secretary of the Interior should examine all existing legislation dealing

46

with such Indians and treaties between the Government of the United States and each such tribe, and report to Congress at the earliest practicable date, but not later than January 1, 1954, his recommendations for such legislation as, in his judgment, may be necessary to accomplish the purpose of this resolution.

Reservation Life and the Need for Proper Education and Training

My people have feelings like the other citizens in the United States and Canada. They bleed when they are cut, they cry when they are hurt, they grow suddenly sad when they are unhappy. Where the difference lies is in the manner by which they express their feelings to the environment and conditions around them. Furthermore, they are citizens with special problems of their own.

The Canadian Indian reservations today, even in the far north, are becoming depleted of game and fish. This will grow progressively worse as the industrialization of the northland takes place, so that the opportunities for hunting and fishing and enjoying the primitive life will grow less and less; consequently, what will my people do? They are beyond the agricultural belt in most cases; they cannot supplement their living by raising vegetables. Vegetables must be bought either as canned goods or goods that come up from the agricultural area. Now, if they have no job opportunity, where are they going to find the money to maintain themselves even at a very low standard of living? The opportunity for them to pursue their former natural way of life is rapidly disappearing and this presents the big problem that is facing my people. Therefore, there is a tremendous need for educating my people and for development of our reservations in both Canada and the United States.

Times are changing. Living in the old ways, the ways of our grandfathers, isn't possible anymore. The Plains Indian can't live by hunting buffalo like he used to, because the wild buffalo are gone.

Many Indians in the northern areas of Canada still try to make a living by hunting and trapping. They spend their lives much as their ancestors did thousands of years before. Most of them are very insular, and not at all integrated into the non-Indian way of life. Quite a number are used as guides by fishing and hunting camp operators. These men still live in the woods and are well versed in woodcraft. But the old ways of hunting and living have for the most part been forgotten; there are few Indians living today who kill deer with a bow and arrow of their own making.

More and more of my people are forced to live by following the white man's way of life, and working at a white man's job. Even if we live close to nature, like the hunters and trappers, we still need money to buy groceries. Some work in fish packing plants, or as miners or loggers, or go berry picking and beet picking. In a few parts of the United States and Canada we still try to follow the old ways. On

49

the West Coast, my people are still fishing much like their ancestors. On the plains, the old buffalo hunters are growing wheat and raising cattle — what my people call the white man's buffalo.

But farming isn't popular today. There are successful Indian farmers and ranchers, but relatively few. There are hundreds of jobs that an Indian could hold, and yet, the number of occupations they actually do follow is much smaller. Sometimes they lack the necessary training. Very often their education is scanty. Sometimes they meet with prejudice and discrimination. Generally, areas in and around reservations are in a depressed state, consequently unemployment on the reservations is high.

When you come into the world of commercial enterprise, particularly in this day of mechanical invention and automation, there are very, very few fields of employment left for the man who has only a strong back to offer. If you're trying to get even a simple job, there must be some means of communication — the ability to speak the English language and also ability to write. Even the simple job of driving a truck, the driver may have the skill to drive the truck; but if he can't read road signs for simple directions, he loses out in the competition for that job.

That's not only an Indian problem. There are other rural inhabitants with the same difficulty. However, for generations, the Indians have had poor education. My people are only just beginning to be able to compete for the jobs.

The average Indian living on reservations doesn't want a steady job. He doesn't want to work week after week, month after month. He doesn't want that. He wants to work for a few days until he gets a paycheck and then spend that before he tries to get any more money. This is a popular point of view, but it's not the whole story. The Indian never accepted the ideas of time, work, or saving. Time was a matter of days and seasons. Work was a matter of building a house or catching fish — not working regular hours for regular wages. Why save for the future when there seemed to be always enough to eat? Sure, these old ideas have to change, but it takes time to catch up with several centuries of white man's progress.

Let's examine the record. What is the white man's progress? The ancient Greeks, from whom western civilization has borrowed so liberally, were intelligent people. In spite of their intelligence and their fertile lands, they were unable to get enough to eat.

The Roman Empire fell in the face of famine. The French were dying of hunger when Thomas Jefferson was president. In mid-1800, the Irish were starving to death; and no one was particularly surprised, because famines on the white man's continent were the rule rather than the exception.

In the 1930s, thousands starved to death in the richest farmlands of the Soviet Union. Hunger has always been normal. Even to this day, the Soviet Union has a wheat shortage. They are ready and willing to take a handout from their rival and world enemy number one — the United States. And the United States is willing and able to underwrite the loss of these grain shipments without using it to their advantage.

If the United States would adopt their Indian Affairs policy as their foreign policy, I should think that we would have the most effective foreign policy since the rise of the Roman Empire.

My people live in many different ways, from having an income of fifteen thousand a year and living in a beautiful suburban bungalow, to living in a cardboard shack on the fringe of a city or town, with no employment and with an income of less than five hundred a year. There's the entire range. Now, there are some people that are in, say, a fringe community with an income of five hundred dollars a year who are on the way up to making a thousand, five thousand a year. These are the ones who left the reservation, the isolation of the lake or of the bush, who are coming to take a look at the world and from there to make a major step into our economy. There are others, however, who are on the fringe settlement, who are on the way back to the reservation, who have come to the major white community, who have not been able to succeed. There are others who feel that they will take a step backward — perhaps to take a stab at it and then become discouraged and go back home or perhaps to say, well, there's nothing at home, there's nothing here, there's nothing in the white community, so I might as well stay where I am — to live and squalor in slums. The United States has spent millions of dollars on its Relocation Program, and as much as one third of those placed on jobs have returned to the reservations.

It is so easy to think of the city Indian as the drunk whom we see in the beer parlor, the skid row bum. Probably because these are the only ones we really see and recognize as Indians.

The Indian who has made the adjustment may be your friend who drives a cab and lives in a small red house in a not-very prosperous part of town. You would not know he was an Indian to look at him, though his wife is rather dark skinned. Generally, they have come from homes on the reservations where they did not have running water or plumbing. Now they have all the amenities, and they don't want to be without them. Of course, they still like to go home to the reservations and visit the old folks, even though they would not go back to outdoor plumbing. In another part of town lives an Indian who may live in a nice, split-level bungalow and have a good position in a big firm. He likes to spend his weekends in his sailboat. He has no relations on the reservation, but he might want to go back there to retire. There are hundreds of Indians living in cities today, and they don't live any differently than non-Indians.

Those of us who leave the reservations to live in the city are likely to find ourselves doing jobs a lot different from the old days. If we don't have a good education, we can't get good jobs any more than the white man. But you'll find us as carpenters, and steelworkers, and technicians, and office workers, and nurses, and so on. Some do well, some don't; just like the white people.

Most Indians live on reservations, some near centers of work, some remote in the country. Probably you'll want to know what they do and how they live. There are all kinds of reservations just as there are all kinds of Indians. All the way from remote areas of wild country occupied by nomadic people living in tents, to tight-knit little communities on the fringe of cities; hardly distinguishable from the rest of the suburbs. Health and living conditions go through the whole range, too. Just about the most primitive people in Canada lived until recently in northern Quebec — nomads — hunting or trapping, living barely above subsistence level. They've been relocated now and placed in houses.

Take the Canadian Nescapis who were at Fort Mac-Kenzie; they lived either in canvas tents or in shacks made with poles and canvas tops. In these shacks, the floors are made with sapling boughs and evergreens. For furniture, they would build some type of a bed off the floor with two-by-fours or something like that, and put boughs again on top, then maybe a sleeping bag. That would be about the only furniture. As for heating and cooking, they would have some type of stove made out of an oil barrel sawed in half, with a piece of tin on top. That would be about the only thing that they would have to cook their meals and warm their dwelling.

As you go further south in Canada, you find the people settling in villages. Still trapping, still living off the land, but not having such a hard time of it. Some reservations in the United States are quite advanced. However, by American standards, they're still pretty primitive.

You could hardly call most reservation dwellings in Canada or the United States modern. They're quite rough. It seems that most of the families sleep on the floor with just numerous blankets under and on top of them. They have quite crude tables and chairs and usually a stove — a cookstove — and very often the house will have only two rooms — one fairly large, and then, directly above it — you go up by a ladder affair — a bedroom. You never find that any of these people undress to go to bed and put on pajamas or anything. They just go to bed in their day clothes; the women mostly in their cloth-covered heads and their moccasins.

And when people live like that, health's a big problem. Living in such squalor, you can be absolutely sure that they're all going to have something wrong with their skin — they're going to have sores. They have a lot of what we call gastroenteritis, and I expect a lot of it is just a lack of hygiene — preparing their food such as it is — and the very unhygienic conditions that they live under. Lack of cleanliness, I would think, is the prime cause of their skin conditions. Just having a good bath once in a while with some good soap and water would help. Very frequently you find that they have just what hospital officials call mechanized dandruff, which is head lice. For a number of our babies, instead of using diapers, the parents will use moss. Now what is moss? It's a light brown color and it looks like dried tobacco. And I'll never forget a story told me about a nurse and an Indian baby who had something wrong with its stomach and bowels. The young nurse was to change the child; she went running to the doctor, absolutely horrified, and she said, that baby *really* had something wrong with it, and the doctor went to look and here it was nothing but moss diapers!

This paints a bad picture, but these situations are in a minority. For the most part, the people living on the reservations are far better off, though few as yet have the

54

amenities we have learned to accept as essentials — indoor plumbing, electric lights, and refrigerators. Some reservations are in the fortunate position of being located in a resort, mining, or lumbering area, so employment opportunities are available. Of course, there are always a few who are not too willing to take advantage of these possibilities, and unfortunately, the outsider usually judges the inhabitants of the reservation by these few. The homes in areas where work is available are modest and well kept. As in any other community, there are those who allow their homes to fall into neglect. Again the outsider will base his judgment of the people on the reservations entirely on the appearance of their homes.

My people think even though they may not have everything on the reservations, it's home and it's theirs. The potential is tremendous for economic growth. They have the sentimental attachment. It's a place that they remember fondly from their youth.

Probably this is the same with all of us. Whatever the standard of living, high or low, the place of our childhood is always home. However, most of the people on the reservations find their whole world there. There are exceptions — Cognawagga, near Montreal, home of the steelworkers who travel all over North America. And there are others. But for the most part, the reservation Indians are quite unsophisticated. World affairs pass them by. They have little interest in reading. They're not even familiar with the provisions of the Indian laws, although they affect them greatly. Back in our schooldays, we learned that Indians were stern, silent people who seldom said more than "Ugh." It's true that it was considered good manners by many of the tribes to keep silent in public, and to speak with deliberation, if they spoke at all. But once the distinguished visitors had left, laughter and jokes were quite general. My people still have a lively sense of humor. They love to laugh, though sometimes their jokes may seem trivial and pointless to the non-Indian.

Judged by non-Indian standards, their speech is often quite uninhibited. They have less regard for convention than some of us are used to, and many of their marriages are common-law. Their families are getting larger now that they no longer lose so many children from ill health. Eight or nine children in a family is quite common.

You'll find the music different in every part of the Indian country. Every group has its own distinctive music. The people on the plains do the old chicken dances, owl dances, grass dances, and so on.

My people's music is beautiful. Our native songs will never leave us. I've been away from the reservation for many years, but I still love the melody. I think our native songs are beautiful. To bring the appreciation of our music, lore, and dancing to the general public, I have initiated a program of Boy Scout Indian Dance teams.

Many Indians are devotedly religious. Many others are completely disinterested. Most of them belong to one or another of the Christian churches — the missionary influence is still very strong — others still adhere to the old beliefs, like the longhouse religion of the Iroquois, and the West Coast secret societies. In 1959, an official Canadian census listed just over 4,000 people holding various "aboriginal beliefs." And just as the so-called pagans love their old sacred music, many of the Christians love to gather together in the home and sing hymns.

I've been generalizing rather a lot, inevitably, and yet there's no single character that fits all Indians. No set pattern to all reservations. Even my people tend to generalize when they talk about themselves, yet there are no two the same.

You see, we don't advance with the times like other American people do. Why don't my people advance like other Americans?

Why did men starve in every century in other parts of the world, yet in America there never has been a famine?

56

Why in this land of plenty are my people on the reservations in the United States and Canada so hard pressed?

Why are the forces of nature harnessed to do the bidding of the humblest citizen? Why is this true for the general population when my people walk and carry goods on their straining backs?

Why, within a few generations, do most Americans take floors, rugs, chairs, tables, chimneys, electric lights, refrigerators, running water, porcelain baths, and toilets as common necessities? Why is the general population so blessed while my people are doing without?

Why are the reservation Indians mostly unwashed, uncombed, with lousy hair, mangy skin, and rotting teeth; when the general population experiences the highest standard of living in the history of mankind?

Why do my people have five times as much gonorrhea, eight times as much hepatitis, ten times as much strep throat, twenty times as much meningitis, and one hundred times as much dysentary as other Americans?

The reasons are not hard to discover. The primitive sanitary conditions under which my people live are in large part responsible for the high disease rate and short life span.

Many thousands of Indians — more than three-fourths of the families on some reservations — have no source of pure water for drinking and household use. They have their water from irrigation ditches or ponds which are often used by livestock and are badly polluted. Also, vast numbers of reservation families lack adequate toilet facilities.

We must make all Americans aware of the fact that they have, right here in their own country, a group of people as deprived as those of any underdeveloped land of Asia or Africa. The incredible thing is that my people happen to be the original owners of this rich continent.

Cultural differences impose a further handicap on health. Medicine men are still active on a number of reservations, and some among my people place greater faith in their charms and potions than in the spotless operating rooms and modern drugs of the white man's Public Health Service.

Transportation is a major problem. Although the United States government maintains over fifty hospitals and forty-two health centers, many patients on the reservations must travel hundreds of miles over primitive roads to reach the nearest medical facility.

What must be done before conditions on the 290 reservations in the United States and the 2,200 reservations in Canada be improved? What must be done to raise my people's standard of living?

We must educate my people — forget about college scholarships — through high school. We must educate all of them, each and every one — young and old. High school graduates run farms, mills, gas stations, drug stores, grocery stores, and the other hundred necessities of everyday life. We need high school graduates — that is our answer, our hope, and our goal. High school graduates are the leaders on our reservations. Therefore, if all were such, then all would be potential leaders.

Along with educating, we must work the land and natural resources of the reservations. We must develop it — economic development.

Every program of the Indian Service should be oriented around educational function. When programs have failed, it has often been because my people were not trained to assume the responsibilities thrust upon them.

A major problem centers around my people's lack of formal education. The median educational level of Indians twenty-five years and older is roughly one-half that of the general non-Indian population. At the college level about one-half of one percent of the Indian population is being enrolled, compared with two percent of the general population. Great strides have been made in Indian education in the past quarter century, but much remains to be done. As the educational level of the general population advances, the gap between Indians and non-Indians will widen, unless the Indian Service increases its efforts to provide educational opportunities for all school-age children, to improve the quality of education through adequate and qualified staffing, and to increase opportunities for adults who have been denied regular schooling.

Integrating Indian youngsters into the public school system should be accomplished wherever possible. Too high a percentage of Indians drop out of school, even in the lower grades. Of those Indians who enter college, few are as well equipped, either in social adjustment or academic preparation, as non-Indians of corresponding age. Many are especially handicapped by the language problem.

In some parts of the country, special summer sessions for Indian students planning to enter college have been instituted on university campuses. The Indian Service should encourage these programs and, where possible, provide a small financial subsidy if one is required. Furthermore, counselling services for Indian students should be improved at all levels.

In addition to problems related to language and other social adjustments, Indian youngsters often leave school because of financial difficulty.

Many of the Indian youngsters who need institutional care should be placed in boarding schools. This is an unfortunate expedient in the field of juvenile affairs.

Because of the heavy financial cost involved in constructing and maintaining school facilities which will accommodate the rapidly expanding Indian school age population, the Indian Service should give serious consideration to using school facilities on a year-round basis, instead of according to the present formula of the 180-day school year. Some system of rotation by semesters, or perhaps an accelerated program, which would permit Indian youngsters to complete their primary and secondary education in fewer than twelve years, would provide fuller utilization of structures and other facilities which are now idle for up to three months each year. However, whenever possible, public facilities should be used.

The added cost of keeping schools running for a full year would be much less than the cost of equivalent new buildings. This proposal has been suggested for the public schools and has been under study by some of the states.

In those areas where facilities are at present sufficient to accommodate all the school age youngsters, the Indian Service should continue its program of using these facilities during the summer months to help Indian children make up educational deficiencies and to assist them with using their leisure constructively. There is a great need everywhere in the Indian country for organized recreational and educational activities to occupy Indian boys and girls during the summer months. Wherever possible, the community and the tribes should work together in setting up such programs. Public school districts should be established on Indian reservations and the ultimate transfer of the Indian Service's educational responsibilities to these districts. Where districts have inadequate tax money to finance a sound school program, the federal government should provide a financial subsidy. Furthermore, it is unrealistic to assume that the states are going to establish more reservation districts so long as the school plants which would be transferred to them by the Indian Service are in poor condition. In order to expedite its program of getting public schools on reservation lands, the federal government must improve the physical plants in which many Indian children are now receiving their education and must also construct new school buildings. Furthermore, it must improve the roads so that Indian children may be transported by bus to these schools. This will eliminate the need for boarding facilities and bring the federal Indian school program more into line with that of the states.

In connection with the establishment of school districts on Indian reservations, the Indian Service must make a greater effort to involve Indian parents in school planning. We must not be satisfied with simply encouraging tribes to form educational committees. The parents of youngsters attending schools must be allowed to participate in the formulation of school programs. Wherever parent-teacher groups have not been formed, they should be established as rapidly as possible. When parents understand what the schools are trying to accomplish, they are more likely to give their support to the educational effort. The goal of the Indian Service should be the ultimate transfer of educational responsibility to local school districts. Therefore, the Indian Service must do everything it can now to help Indian parents learn of their rights and duties with respect to schools. The time to begin providing them with such assistance is not after the transfer, but before.

Where federal schools continue to operate on Indian reservations, the Indian Service should insist that children of government employees attend these schools along with the Indian youngsters. When the Indian Service on the one hand strongly advocates the integration of Indian and non-Indian youngsters in the public schools and, on the other, permits segregation through discouraging non-Indians from enrolling in schools which it maintains, its policies appear inconsistent.

Since one of the major problems in educating Indian youngsters stems from the fact that English is often not their home language, the Indian Service has the important responsibility of keeping abreast of the latest developments in language training and instructing its educational personnel in these procedures. An in-service training program is essential in this area and should be conducted in conjunction with the universities and colleges located nearby. In states where minority languages exist, the state teachers' colleges have been dealing with problems related to lan-

61

guage training for Mexican-Americans and Indians for many years and, doubtless, have courses, seminars and workshops of great potential value to Indian Service education personnel.

Finally, because of the many problems peculiar to Indian education, and because policies have been changing rapidly, an education survey should be made. Such a survey should include not merely formal schoolwork, but the impact of the changing policies on the community and the children.

Indian education should afford the individual the opportunity of being educated to his full capacity. The schools which my people attend, whether federal, public or private, should have the best curricula, programs, teaching methods and guidance used in white education, modified and augmented to meet the special requirements of Indian students. The quality of instruction the Indian student receives and its adaptation to his needs should be the prime consideration.

The support of the Indian community, its neighbors, and local government officials should be enlisted for the attainment of these goals.

In reaching these objectives, the education division of the Indian Service should consider, on the one hand, the variations between groups, areas, Indian cultures, and the attitudes of adjacent communities, including the existence or absence of discrimination against the Indian child. On the other hand, the quality of the teaching staff and their ability to cope with the special difficulties of the student and his parents should be directed to the goal of imparting knowledge without destroying the moral influences and restraints of the child's family and culture.

In no case should public schools attended by my people be required to lower their standards. Pains should be taken by all the authorities concerned to avoid any friction which might result from the additional financial burden put on the non-Indian taxpayer by educating Indians in public schools.

The problems raised by taking Indian youngsters from their homes to live in large dormitories, so as to enable them to attend public schools in cities, should be evaluated in terms of the individual's age, his emotional adjustment, and a consideration of his home life.

In making arrangements for attendance of reservation Indians at public schools, the federal government, in fulfillment of its obligations, should require that adequate standards be maintained. If standards drop, the federal government should no longer allocate money to the school.

The educational duty of the United States does not diminish the obligations of the states, under their constitutions and laws, to educate my people on a parity with their own citizens.

On the basis of the above criteria, Indian pupils should be divided into three general classes according to their capacity and background:

(a) Those who will profit from public school: in general, this group would include pupils from an English-speaking stable family which has adopted the white culture in place of its Indian heritage.

(b) Those who will profit from a federal school: these would be pupils chosen from unassimilated families because, among other things, they are unable to speak or to understand English.

(c) Those for whom both federal and public education should be considered.

For the Indian child in group (b) or (c), the following should be provided: early and continuous training in English; instruction in the history, culture and accomplishments of the Indians; training in arts and crafts; teachers qualified to teach both English as a second language and Indian culture; the motivating of students of different languages and cultural backgrounds; special subjects that Indian children require, such as handling money, etc.

Teachers so qualified should have adequate compensation. Those in the federal service should have a work year equivalent in length to that customary in public schools. Besides teacher training, all those in contact with the Indian children — bus drivers, dormitory attendants, and teachers' aides — should have special training.

Children should have counseling through grade and high school. Vocational training should be supplied to those proposing to enter a trade. For those qualified to attend college, suitable instruction should be given to equip them to enter and remain there. Counseling should continue through the college years.

Training should have as one of its continuing objectives to discover and enable pupils who show special promise to move into higher education and by this means qualify for executive positions either inside or outside the tribe.

Adequate scholarships, grants, and loans should be provided by the United States to my people where needed.

Education for adults should be strengthened to include more subjects, as well as the use of T.V. and other modern techniques, and be extended to more reservations.

A strong parent-teacher relationship should be developed and community schools reestablished; consultation of school authorities with tribal leaders should be facilitated.

Mission schools should be encouraged to continue to supply their share of the leadership.

The Indian parent must see that his child attends school regularly and should encourage him to do well in his studies.

Where compulsory attendance laws do not exist in a tribe it should take action to have such legislation enacted and enforced.

Money for building schools and the repair of dilapidated ones should be supplied.

Among families in a low-income bracket, provision for economic improvement should go hand in hand with education.

Per capita payments should occur, when funds are available, in September and December.

Indian Origin: Where, When, Why and How

Now let's turn back the calendar and examine some of the early influences of my people, in the years before the white man's influence began to change him — or rather — tried to change him.

The way of the Indian country has changed a lot since the old days. None of us can remember what things were like before the white man came, but our grandfathers used to say that they were a lot better off.

I wonder how many people know much about the early history of their own race. Certainly my people have little or no written knowledge of theirs. For one thing they have no written records. Then again, even the scientists are only beginning to come to a general agreement about the origin of the Indian. At least these findings account for some of the early inhabitants of the western world. Indian mythology tells us many interesting things. For instance, it tells us of the mysterious arrival of a group of religious leaders who might well be the Nephites. It tells of the great builders who came to Central and South America to engineer the building of the magnificent structures found there. Therefore, without written records it is impossible to be adamant about any one origin of the American Indian. They could hardly have come from the same culture, because there were several highly advanced cultures among the early inhabitants here. Suffice it to say that my interpretation of the evidence is as authentic as anyone else's.

In the light of present archaeological and scientific findings, it has been shown that three groups of people, their culture full-blown, arrived by sea and landed in the vicinity of Central America. This is in accordance with the discovery of ancient historical writings and carbon-14 determinations. One such migration occurred between 2000-3000 B.C. from Central Asia, and two others in 600 B.C. from the Near East, having strong influences of Mesopotamian, Egyptian, and Hebrew culture.

Perhaps the most impressive and thought-provoking account of the origin of the American Indian is to be found in *The Book of Mormon*. The Mormons (i.e., members of The Church of Jesus Christ of Latter-Day Saints) claim this divine book to be none other than the record or "stick" of Joseph, as mentioned by the Prophet Ezekial to be a companion book to the record of Judah (the Jews) which the world recognizes as the Holy Bible.

The Book of Mormon contains accounts of three groups of people who migrated to the American continent. The first was in very ancient times, corresponding to the time of the Tower of Babel incident as recorded in the Bible. The account gives us second witness concerning the tower and how God, in his wrath, caused confusion and changes in the language and understanding of the people. Some of those who were involved in that great calamity were blessed by a prophet who, under the direction of the Lord, led them, even like Moses who was later to lead a chosen people of the Lord to a land of promise. Under this prophet, who is identified simply as the brother of Jared, the people were led to the shores of the ocean, where they received divine instruction in the building of ships, which brought them to their land of promise — the Americas.

The Book of Mormon tells of another group of people who left the land of Jerusalem during the first year of the reign of Zedekiah, king of Judah (600 B.C.). Here again we find a spiritual leader, Lehi, a prophet and descendant of Joseph who was sold into Egypt, having been warned in a vision of the impending destruction of Jerusalem, taking his family and a few friends and departing under divine guidance. Only a few years later another group left the Near East. Both groups came to America and later merged.

There was a serious split in the Prophet Lehi's family which resulted in the growth of two great, yet bitterly opposed, nations, known as the Nephites and Lamanites. Here is recorded the writings of American prophets, statesmen, and historians. Here we glimpse the ancient customs, governments, intrigues, industry, beliefs, feelings, rivalry, and the devastating wars which raged between these mighty empires.

Perhaps the greatest single incident is that of the visitation of the resurrected Christ in which he taught the people many wonderful things and mercifully healed their sick and afflicted.

It is believed that many of the Indians of the Americas are descendants of the Lamanites, and that all are of a noble lineage. They received the promise that they would never entirely be destroyed and more, that they would someday enter a state of prominence and honor among all peoples — a delightsome and highly favored people of the Lord.

Here is the legend: many, many years ago in the beginning of time, a hunter stood on the shores of the Bering

Straits. One day he was taken captive by another hunter and in his distress he called on his guardian spirit for help. At once the cave in which he was confined was torn open and he was set free. "Go forth," he was told, "go forth ever eastwards. Turn your back on the sea where your enemies are."

"Let us both travel towards the sunrise," he suggested, and he and his guardian spirit set out on a long trail across Alaska and the Yukon, down into the vast plains and mountains of Canada and America. And in the years that followed thousands more trod the same path.

Those are only a few legends that we have about the Indian's arrival in America. This question of where the Indians came from has been puzzling the Indian and the white man for a long time.

There has been a lot of strange suggestions and ideas as to where the Indians came from. Therefore, it is not surprising that only comparatively recently has science had a meeting of the minds.

No serious anthropologist disputes that the Indians came from the eastern hemisphere. In fact it is quite certain that man did not evolve on this continent. There is not a shred of evidence for supposing that the American Indian originated in the New World. No modern or fossil forms of primitive man have ever been found here, and yet many thousands of fossil-bearing geological formations have been investigated, both in North and South America.

We will concede that some Indian people could have come across the Bering Straits. It is only about fifty miles across, and there are islands halfway where they could camp. The far shore can easily be seen on a clear day. It is a possible route actually and it is the only route to which there is no serious objection. Actually, Mongoloid people still live on both sides of the straits, and it is still in use as a migration route. The Eskimos of western Alaska have friends and relatives in Eastern Siberia. They speak the same language and they cross back and forth despite the objections of Soviet officials.

69

Some people think that there was a land bridge, which is quite probable when we consider the large mammals that crossed over. But if there were such a bridge, that was a long time before man began to cross from the Old World to the New.

Even if there were a land bridge that man used, why did they cross? After all, these were hunting people. It is probable that they moved into northern Asia in the first place because of the superabundance of game there. Once they could get across into the New World, where food was even more plentiful and the climate was more inviting, they decided to stay.

It is generally felt that some migration from the Old World to the New began about twenty thousand years ago. Of course we are prepared for new evidence; it could shift the date one way or the other; but it is almost certain, in fact, it is quite certain, that they crossed over without any realization at all that they were invading a new continent. It was merely another piece of land that they could see, and they simply hopped over the straits and found it good and stayed. It wasn't just one big migration. It is felt quite strongly now that there were many waves of migrants. We don't know how many, but there were certainly several of them, and we don't know what intervals separated these various waves.

One family might come over this week, another one a few days later. There might be a pause of another three years. I don't suppose there ever was a group of five or six thousand people waiting on one side saying, "We'll come over next Saturday afternoon," or anything of that sort.

This idea of a series of waves of migration, if you like to call them that, partially explains the great variety that we find in the racial backgrounds of the people that are found here now. There are a great many differences in their physical appearances, in their culture, and in their languages, for instance.

70

You cannot tell, of course, which languages were spoken by the prehistoric Indians, but in Canada, for example, there are at least fifty separate languages spoken by the Indians. In the United States, this figure would run into the hundreds. They aren't just slightly different languages like English and Dutch; they are, in many cases, very, very different, like English and Chinese. Especially on the West Coast there was an even greater variety. On the West Coast, for example, it is not unusual for people who live just a few miles apart from each other to be quite unable to understand each other's speech. It is not possible that all of these languages developed from the same group of people migrating from Asia. Therefore, the position that the American Indian has several places of origin is fortified.

In skin, eye and hair color, Indians are like the Mongoloids, the South Sea Islander, and the Asiatic Indians.

Where did the Europeans come from before they settled in Europe? Or the Africans, or the Asiatics? The dogmatic approach of so-called experts is amazing when it comes to answers to questions concerning my people.

There are authorities on early man in the New World who say that we must not get any impression of masses of people moving swiftly across the straits and marching briskly down the continent in search of a more pleasant climate, or in pursuit of animals that were rushing south. That is very far from the true picture. Perhaps it is unfortunate that the word *migration* has been used in the first place; a better word would be *diffusion*.

There may have been pressure from behind, a scarcity of game, a tendency to wander and roam, a desire to explore the new land. The newcomers just spread as mist spreads in a valley or clouds drift across the sky. In the course of time, they wandered right down to Tierra Del Fuego, in fact, at the very southern tip of South America, and out to the Pacific Islands.

There seems to be more and more evidence challenging

71

old beliefs and supporting new ones on the kinship of the South Sea Islander and the American Indian. Thor Heyerdahl, Norwegian anthropologist, in his book, *American Indians in the Pacific,* points out this kinship.

The great stone pyramids in Mexico, Central America, and South America are almost identical in structure, plan, and material (if not in size) as those found in the South Sea Islands. Stone roadways, so characteristic of the pre-Inca period of America, are found to be duplicated in some of the Pacific Islands. Giant stone statues such as are found in South America are now being discovered in the Polynesian Islands (according to Mark E. Peterson).

When you add the multiple migrations to the South Sea Islands, populating the Americas over an extended period of thousands of years isn't too great a task.

It seems like a long way, but if you do a little figuring on it, it is not so far. Even if the straits were the only route, it could be done. If you have a group of people and they moved steadily south at the rate of only one mile a week, starting in western Alaska, it would take them less than two hundred and fifty years to reach the southern tip of South America. Not that any group ever actually did this of course, but it just shows that it is not that far and that it wouldn't necessarily take all that time.

With twenty thousand years to play in, we can easily afford two hundred and fifty. But, naturally, they never moved at any such speed. The people living in this stage of culture obtained their food by hunting and fishing, gathering nuts and seeds and roots and berries and shellfish, and so on. They had no agriculture, no weaving, no pottery. They didn't know the bow and arrow, which wasn't invented until a good deal later. They lived a sort of semi-nomadic existence, wandering around in search of food, living in temporary dwellings or rock shelters. But in certain good localities where there was an abundance of shellfish or other easily obtainable food, they settled down to more or less permanent settlements.

72

If by nomad you mean one who wanders continuously and has no fixed place of abode, the Indian was not one. In fact there are very few true nomads anywhere in the world. Each Indian tribe or band had its own boundaries, known at least to the elders and the neighboring Indian tribes. Within these bounds some people followed a regular round of activities, fishing here at one season, going on to another place for berry picking, onto another sheltered area to pass the winter, off to another spot to dig bulbs in the spring, and so on. Out on the West Coast the boundaries of clover and berry patches, fishing stations, clam diggings were well defined and the ownership well known. And in the east the boundaries of trap lands were well established; even on the Plains boundaries were well known. They often fought over them, too, though they might be just vague limitations like the east side of a range of hills or one or the other bank of a river.

Perhaps they weren't true nomads in the strict sense, but they certainly were mobile. This is reflected in the type of housing, in most cases probably only skin stretched over poles, cut on the spot and left standing when the people moved on. And in some parts of Canada, for example, the Northwest Territories, things haven't changed much even now.

Indian houses, in fact, varied greatly depending on the climate of the area, the occupations of the people, and so on. In the northern woods where hunting and fishing were the means of livelihood, the home had to be portable. They used what we generally call a wigwam, a temporary shelter in which conifer branches or woven mats or perhaps sheets of birch bark were used to cover a conical or domed framework of poles. When the people moved away, they took the mats of birch bark or sheets with them and left the poles standing, knowing that there would be others at the next camping place.

But in the more permanent villages, houses were sometimes quite large and accommodated several families in each. These were sturdy erections of poles covered with large sheets of elm bark, which in this case, would stand for many years. The Plains Indians used a tepee, much like a wigwam, except for the fact that the poles were covered with hides, usually buffalo, and the poles and hides were both taken along when the people moved. Poles were hard to come by in the treeless Plains. It was a familiar saying that a good set of tepee poles was worth more than a woman.

In the Columbia Plateau, they weren't quite so mobile, especially in the wintertime, because their winter houses were built underground. These were big, circular holes, roofed with a conical roof of logs covered over with turf. They were very warm and stuffy, but they were much more comfortable than the forty-below weather outside. In summer, of course, they were mobile. They had portable shelters of woven matting. The biggest native houses were on the West Coast. Some of these enormous buildings were so large that young men used to run races inside. The main structure of these were big cedar logs for the post and the beams, with roofs and walls made out of split cedar planks. Many of these were carved with painted house fronts and totem poles standing outside.

It was real architecture and certainly the highest in Canada; not by any means the highest in the Americas, of course. Further south, down Mexico way and South America, the people, although they are still Indians in the true sense, had gone a great deal further along the path of civilization. They had developed agriculture, weaving, pottery, architecture, mathematics, astronomy. They would even predict an eclipse of the sun and the moon. But elsewhere on the continent the Indians found some places were a good deal more liveable than others and intended to stay there.

No matter how crude or primitive his tribal organization was, there were two things at least on which he pinned his living and conduct. One was respect for the old people, who through experience and perhaps inherent wisdom, made decisions, after consultation with the braves or the tribe. Nonetheless, the elders were the leaders. The other factor was the principle of democracy, i.e., the leaders consulted with the council of the tribe.

What I find very different and practically gone from my people today is the lectures they used to get from their parents and the elders of the tribe.

Men were chosen by the chiefs of the camp, who would go around in the morning and at night telling the people what their chief tells them to do, and a lot of them respectfully complied.

The Indian did not have the acquisitive sense of the European — in other words, pride of possession. His prestige came rather from his skill as a hunter, his courage as a warrior, or perhaps his wisdom and eloquence. They had secret societies and rituals that governed their conduct. Things were taboo not for any reason other than they had found that there were certain things you just did not do.

That was about the state of things when the first white man arrived, a fairly high degree of civilization in the most favored areas and a much lower standard elsewhere. There seems to be another popular misconception here that my people were engaged in constant fighting. Actually, fighting between the tribes wasn't nearly as prevalent as some of our schoolbooks might suggest. It wasn't until they got firearms that it became more serious. The only thing they didn't kill — well, if they liked the woman — they'd take her for themselves. In the first place, here was another tribe, another kind of people who spoke a different language. They would go out and try to capture their horses and the other tribes would do the same. However, when they did fight neighbor tribes, they really fought, and took few prisoners.

War, as an organized attack of one large body of men

on another, was almost impossible anywhere in the Indian country, for these people had little in the way of reserves of food. Therefore, they couldn't keep an army in the field if the men had to go off hunting every day or so. When the French and English were engaged in military campaigns, they were able to feed their Indian allies at least in part, because of their experience in feeding large bodies of men on the march. However, first contact between the white people and the Indian was friendly enough. The early explorers referred constantly to the friendly welcome offered them by the natives.

This was due in part, at least, to what mythology tells us was the "Second Coming." There was a great man who glowed as if he were possessed of the sun. This man came from on high to bring a message to his flock that they too were of great importance in the scheme of things physical and spiritual. Therefore, little wonder when the white man came; for the most part, he was received in a friendly manner. And he was so treated as long as he deserved or earned it.

Little wonder, then, when the fur traders pushed into the Oregon country, my people were charmed by the religion of the Catholic Iroquois. This was as early as the 1820s. My people, then and now, think of the white man's religion as good medicine with great power.

In the 1830s, my people of the Oregon country sent a delegation to St. Louis to learn more about Christianity. Among the able Christian leaders were Marcus Whitman, Henry Spalding, and Father Pierre De Smet. These fine men began to spread the word of God through the Oregon country.

De Smet established a mission in the Flathead area. Other Jesuits did the same throughout the Oregon country and Canada. In fact the Christian missions and mission schools so impressed my people that at the Twentieth Annual Convention of the U. S. National Congress of American Indians meeting at Bismark, North Dakota in September 1963, they passed the following resolutions:

RESOLUTION I

Whereas the Christian mission schools have been conducted for the education of the Indian people since the 16th century, and whereas the mission schools were the only schools which took care of Indian education until late in the 19th century; and whereas many of the delegates present here today received their training in these mission schools; be it resolved, that The National Congress of American Indians goes on record as commending the work of the mission schools.

Little wonder that in 1536 Jacques Cartier recorded: "And we, having arrived at the said Hochelaga, more than a thousand persons presented themselves before us, men, women and children alike, that which gave us a good reception as ever father did to child, showing marvelous joy. For the men in one band danced, the women on their side and the children on the other, the which brought us store of fish and of their bread made of coarse millet which they cast into our aid boats in a way that it seemed as if it tumbled from the air."

The way of life of the average Indian before white contact was remarkably like that of out-of-door people anywhere else. The women looked after the children, made the clothing and prepared and cooked the food, did the weeding and harvesting if they grew corn, tanned the hides and made the pottery. That sounds like an unfair division of labor until we reflect that the white man did about the same thing, and still does. The men of course, hunted and fished, set traps, skinned the game, looked after the safety of the camp and its inhabitants. We must remember that hunting and fishing were not sport as they are today. They were dangerous and tiring work that had to be carried on, day after day, from the time the man was first able to go

77

on the trail until he died or became too feeble to hunt any more.

Whenever we think of Indians hunting we think of the buffalo. Of course, the question arises of why the buffalo became extinct. The Indian and the buffalo existed side by side for thousands of years. There was no thought of extinction of this animal; it roamed the plains in millions. The hunting of the Indians undoubtedly destroyed thousands, especially the method they had of buffalo jumps, in which whole herds were chased over a cliff and many hundreds were killed. But this had been going on for thousands of years, and it wasn't a deciding factor in the extinction of the buffalo. It was the introduction of the gun in the hands of both the whites and the Indians that turned the balance and made the survival of the buffalo impossible.

However, before the ink dried in good old American gun on the part of the white man was the only factor. Another one we must include was alcohol, which was important in the decay of the ancient Indian cultures. Since the sixteen hundreds, unscrupulous trappers and adventurers of all sorts had been teaching the Indians to drink spirits, particularly rum, in order to destroy their bargaining capabilities.

In 1750, the Hudson Bay fur trader, Ischam reported... "These natives are given very much to quarreling when in liquor, having known two brothers when in liquor to quarrel after such a manner that they bit one another's nose, ears and fingers off, biting being common with them when in liquor, and no poison so venomous as their teeth. They also were very sulky, sullen, and if at any time one has a resentment against another they never show it till the spiritous liquors work in their brains, then they speak their mind freely."

Out on the West Coast things were different. White contact, except for the most casual and short visits of which we know little or nothing, dates pretty well from the arrival of Captain Cook on the coast in 1778 when he made his almost continuous survey as far north as the Bering Straits. I wonder if Captain Cook knew that he was being watched from the shore.

Chief Maquinna and Chief Nanaimis saw three sticks on the horizon which came closer and closer. "It's some sort of a canoe," said Maquinna; "a big canoe with white wings. It goes fast and makes great waves. It must be the Sisiutl that moves it, the double-headed snake." Quickly they launched a canoe with strong young men to paddle it and the woman witch doctor standing in the boat shaking her rattle and singing "Hai, great canoe salmon, Hai, Hai, great spring salmon. We greet you, we welcome you." Then Chief Maquinna followed her in his canoe holding his spear in his hand and singing loudly. "I am Maquinna," he cried. "My village is near and a good safe anchorage. I want you to stay as my guest. I will treat you well." And he gave Captain Cook the fine sea otter skin robe he was wearing, and Captain Cook gave him his cocked hat, all covered with gold braid; and the Captain and the Chief lived together as friends.

Captain Cook would agree that this is just about as it did happen, though he wrote of it in different words: "April 1778. The coasts appear to be inhabited by a race of people whose inoffensive behavior promised friendly intercourse. At their first coming they generally went through a singular mode of introducing themselves. They would paddle with all their strength quite round both ships. The Chief, or some other principal person in the canoe, standing up with a spear or some other weapon in his hand and speaking or rather hollering all the time. Sometimes the orator of the canoe would have his face covered with a mask representing either a human visage or that of some animal. And instead of a weapon would hold a rattle in his hand. Our friends, the natives attended us until we were almost out of the sound. Some on board the ships and others in the canoes. One of their chiefs was among the last who left us, having before he went, bestowed upon him a small present, I received in return a beaver skin of much greater value. Struck with this instance of generosity, so I presented him a new broadsward with a brass hilt, the possession of which made him completely happy."

One thing in Canada and northern United States, of course, was of urgent importance — clothing. When it gets forty and fifty below you had to have clothes. And at the time of the white contact, my people mostly dressed in tanned skins. Back east it was generally deer skin, or buck skin as we call it. On the prairies, they liked caribou skin. On the West Coast they wore furs, and a good deal of clothing was made of shredded cedar bark. Their clothing was strictly functional. It was intended to keep you warm or to impress the beholder. Modesty just didn't enter into it. Some Indians wore as little as possible, going with no clothes at all if the weather was hot. The women often wore nothing above the waist. The children ran about naked until their early teens, except in cold weather. Some of the painted and decorated clothes of the prairie Indians, by the way, were extremely handsome garments.

Morals, both in the way of dress, which was purely functional, and in such matters as premarital freedom, plurality of wives, wife lending, multiple intercourses in religious ceremonies, all of them seem lax by our standards. Yet there was a high standard of manners, a definite code of ethics which had to be adhered to, such as treatment of guests, for example.

Alexander Henry, in 1806, was most impressed. "Just before we entered the village we were met by the chief of the place 'Chat Noir' and a number of the natives. Everyone shook hands and bade us welcome as we rode on through their ranks. The chief then conducted us to one of his huts which was appropriated for the reception of the strangers. He even keeps one of his wives in this house we

80

entered, to wait upon his guests, cook, bring water and even serve as a bedfellow when required. On going into the hut we found buffalo hides spread on the ground before the fire for us to sit upon. We were presented with two large dishes of boiled corn and beans. After that they gave us a large dish of boiled dried meat, but few of us could eat it as it had too strong a smell and taste."

But this state of affairs wasn't to continue. The white man with his so-called civilizing influence had to change the old order. By the early eighteen hundreds, the immigrant settlers were firmly established and so were their civilized customs.

Alexander Henry's journal continues, "January 1st, 1811. This being the first day of another year, our people have passed it according to the custom of the Indians in drinking and fighting. Some of the principal Indians desired us to allow them to remain at the fort that they might see our people drink. As soon as they began to be a little intoxicated and to quarrel among themselves, well the natives began to be apprehensive that something might befall them also. They therefore hid themselves under the beds and elsewhere saying that they thought the white people had gone mad and they appeared not to know what they were about."

The advantages of civilization, the white man's influence — has it been all bad? Would the Indians have been better off without these benefits? Yet, with the most advanced civilization of all time flanking my people on every side, they remain as grimly deprived as those of any underdeveloped land of Asia and Africa.

From the outset, the governments of Canada and the United States did not consider my people as full citizens. In isolated cases, this is still the practice of local governments. Because of this and other injustices, my people were never really aware of the fact that they were a part of government; and, the hard core of that fact many

81

white people seem to be forgetting: namely, no government can support its people, for the simple reason that a government must derive its support from the people.

In the final analysis, where and when and why and how the Indian came to the western hemisphere has little bearing on his present condition. The Indian, as an individual and as a tribe, is what should concern those who want to help him to better his lot. There is no excuse and no reason why my people should not enjoy the same standard of living as the general population.

However, if my people do not want to live as they do — if they do not want to be always in destitution, always on the verge of starvation — they must come to realize that they, and they alone, can control their destiny. Much help will come from the government, the churches, and service groups. However, the men who make up the groups are only men, and no man can control another's thoughts, speech, or creative actions.

Health Needs On Reservation and Off Reservation

Similar to the Chewing Blackbones' tradition, in the spring of 1963 in the Yukon an old Indian died. He was called Copper Joe. When he was a boy his parents used to make knives, skin scrappers, and arrowheads out of native copper found in the stream beds. When the Alaska highway pushed through within a few yards of his cabin, he revived the old copper industry and sold his work as souvenirs and curios to construction men, soldiers, tourists, and anybody else who would buy them. This is how he came to be called Copper Joe. His son, a bright boy, didn't take to working in copper; instead he learned to drive a caterpillar. He makes good wages working on highway construction. He wears white man's clothes, speaks English well, eats white man's food. He has made the transition from the copper age to the atomic age in one generation, and this same transition, in spite of all our advantages, has taken the white man more than three thousand years.

Probably there are not many Copper Joes left today, and for the most part it takes several generations for the Indian to make the change from the copper age. Several generations of painful experiences taught him that every white man can't be trusted. Trust, to my people, is an important part of life.

Of course, the difficult thing that confronted my people was the unscrupulousness of some white men. I do not know how much pride the average citizen takes in his early ancestry; I'm thinking of the European civilization now. Many of their ancestors were landless and lawless men who were evicted from their own home countries and arrived in a land where no law existed, other than the law of power and strength. It is no wonder that they rode roughshod over the Indian population in the early days. They found that for a cask of rum, firewater, for example, the Indian would give up anything. Under the influence of alcohol my people would agree to anything. This was what brought out degradation and moral deterioration, because the Indian, once having given his word, abided by it. His favorite expression was that "he did not talk with a forked tongue." In other words, he did not say one thing and mean another.

There were a lot of other things too. You take Newfoundland. They exterminated all the Indians there for one reason or another. The main reason was probably because that was the place where all the pirates came. They weren't satisfied with pirating on the seas so they pirated the natives of that country.

The Beothuks of Newfoundland were deliberately exterminated. First by another tribe, the Micmacs, and then

84

by the white settlers. There was a bounty on their scalps and they were hunted down like vermin. The last of their race, a slave servant girl, died in 1829. In the New England states there were bounties for Indian scalps too, any Indian scalps. In 1755 a man's scalp brought 20 pounds sterling; a woman's or male child's brought 20 pounds sterling. In 1756 the price jumped to 300 pounds sterling for the scalp of every enemy. Fortunately, these were isolated incidents among the early settlers, and by 1756 the Indians had adopted the white man's ways so much that one historian reported:

> The North American Indian had, within one generation of contact with the fur trader, become so utterly dependent on European firearms for hunting that the Company was fully justified in claiming that many thousand families of the natives for want of the supply, they annually received from us of guns, powder and shot wherewith they killed beaver, buffalo and several other beasts of that country, the flesh whereof is their food, would be starved before the next year. And Governor Jeremy left a tragic account of the starvation, cannibalism and infanticide caused by this lack of trading goods. For they have lost their skill with the bow since Europeans have supplied them with firearms.

Once my people learned to depend on firearms instead of the bow and arrow, other problems arose. Warfare between the various tribes increased so much that the Hurons were all but wiped out. Fighting between Indians and white settlers became worse. In the peaceful areas, the Indian was able to kill all the game wantonly. Before, he killed only enough for his needs. Now he killed for the sake of killing; consequently, the buffalo and the caribou became scarce. So it was my people's ability to adapt themselves to the white man's way that resulted in our becoming completely dependent. We forgot how to make bows or tan hides. We adopted the white man's dress. We traded with the settlers and bought our food instead of hunting like in the old days.

There were other results just as serious. There was disease. We know about the number of medicine men and from the many herbal remedies that there must have been plenty of sickness among the Indians, but it seems likely that many of the diseases common in Europe were unknown here. So the Indians had little resistance. Once smallpox appeared amongst the Montagnais of Quebec, in about 1635, it spread across the Indian country to the Rockies like a flood. Wave after wave of smallpox swept the country, and travelers told of finding tepees with every soul within lying dead. Tuberculosis and measles, too, were terrible killers among the Indian population. Today, medical science has reduced these until they are no longer a major problem.

Even though there have been substantial improvements in Indian health since World War II, Indian death rates continue higher than the national average. The Indian life span is approximately two-thirds that of the general American population, and the infant mortality rate is about two times as high.

Indians generally agree that health services have been more effective since they were transferred to the Department of Health, Education and Welfare. This situation partially is attributable to the fact that the latter department has had a larger appropriation and more medical specialists at its disposal than did the Indian Service.

There should be effective communication at top levels between all departments affecting Indians and the Indian Service. There should be high-policy groups composed of representatives of all departments that affect Indians, and these groups should meet regularly to make sure that objectives, programs and policies are consistent.

There is a need for water and sewage disposal systems, hospitals and clinics, and in some areas, health educators and medical social workers. The lack of water and sewage disposal systems is especially serious. There should be a training program to prepare Indian communities for assuming the responsibility of maintaining water and sewage disposal systems once they have been installed.

There should not be payment for health services provided Indians, even from those Indians who can afford to contribute to the cost of their own medical care. This policy would be applicable to Indians living on reservations.

Health services to off reservation Indians should be provided on an 80%-20% basis, the government giving 80% and the Indians paying 20%. Relocatees and migratory laborers are especially vulnerable, as they are often unable to secure locally administered services, and are restricted from using those provided by the federal government.

My people should receive adequate medical care. This, for maximum results, should be supplemented with improved education and economic betterment. Funds allocated for hospitals, medical personnel, and general health services should bear a proper relation to those appropriated for other purposes.

In some areas, federal, state and local health agencies need to be coordinated, and local specialists used. In others, a closer cooperation between the Public Health Service and the Indian Service should be established to ensure that the national policy for Indian development and welfare is effective and consistent. Funds should be made available to improve roads and telephones to clinics and hospitals.

Sanitary water and sewer systems should be increased. They should be installed in coordination with housing and like programs. Pains should be taken to eliminate duplication in the construction, operation, and administration of these undertakings.

The United States Public Health Service, despite its excellent record of performance, should adjust traditional professional attitudes and practices to make them more suitable and acceptable to my people. The doctor should

87

treat patients not only as individuals but also as constituent members of a group, a group which may sharply differ both culturally and linguistically from a white community. He should confer with my people and seek when possible to benefit from their counsel.

In view of the historic responsibility of the United States for Indian health, the Public Health Service should not agree with states to relinquish services without prior consultation with the tribes to be affected.

When the tribes approve such transfer, the government should set enforceable standards to assure the quality and continuation of the services, and prevent discrimination against my people.

Preventive medicine, and maternal and child health should be stressed. Effective cooperation between the Public Health Service and schools, whether federal or state, should be obtained. Public health nurses should be made directly responsible to the physicians in charge, and doctors and nurses and hospital administrators should increase their use of Indian personnel whenever possible.

The tribes, for their part, should assume greater responsibility for health and sanitation. To this end, my people should learn to recognize those common diseases which demand immediate attention. Both adults and children should be educated by health agencies to take the first steps when illness strikes, and the agencies should make it possible for patients lacking transportation to get to hospitals and clinics. Furthermore, the schools should provide instruction in sanitation and nutrition for both children and adults.

The categorical aids (for the care of the aged, the blind, dependent children and the permanently and totally disabled) in the United States are administered by states to both reservation and off reservation Indians on the same basis as to other citizens. The Indian Service, through its branch of Welfare, provides general assistance to Indians living within the boundaries of a reservation and on other trust or restricted land (except in a few states which include reservation Indians in their own programs and in parts of Oklahoma and Alaska, where the Indian Service's general assistance program is extended to certain other Indians as well).

In many states, the general assistance program is wholly or largely financed and administered by counties whose budgets are limited. It is common practice for such counties to employ legal devices designed to keep down the welfare load. Persons may be excluded from eligibility for a variety of reasons related in some way to residence. In states with large Indian populations, such as the Dakotas, certain rules effectively exclude off reservation Indians from entitlement to state and county assistance. It may be true that other persons besides Indians are excluded, but in some counties far more Indians than non-Indians are affected.

The Indian Service has consistently taken the position in recent years that off reservation Indians are entitled to the same state and county services as are other inhabitants of the areas in which they live. Furthermore, it maintains that to provide general welfare assistance to those living off the reservation gives the states and counties additional excuse for excluding Indians from the general assistance programs which they maintain.

Although there have been few cases in which the Indian Service's contention has been tested, those which have reached the courts have resulted in decisions favoring the Indian Service's position. Yet, in spite of these favorable decisions, testimony by Indians indicates that some counties and states are still excluding Indians from general welfare assistance simply saying to them, "You're not eligible. Go back to the reservation and the federal government will take care of you."

In arguing against assuming the responsibility for off reservation Indians, some states and counties often maintain that these Indians represent a welfare burden they cannot afford financially; that the Indians were placed by the federal government on reservations with limited resources which the Indian Service has not always aided the tribes in developing; and that the Indians, because of federal neglect, are not sufficiently educated or skilled to provide themselves with incomes adequate for subsistence. Although these arguments in many cases reflect a measure of truth, the federal government has insisted that the states and counties have the same responsibilities to Indians as to others, regardless of historical circumstances, and that a federal subsidy for off reservation Indians should be provided only when it is provided for other citizens as well.

The problem of general assistance for off-reservation Indians is one which has three facets:

1. Who has the legal responsibility for providing welfare services?
2. If it is determined that states and counties have the responsibility, is federal assistance needed because of low-income level locally? (If such assistance is needed, it should come preferably in a form which does not treat Indians as a separate group.)
3. Pending such determinations, how should interim assistance be provided?

In the old days, medicine, health, and welfare were not complicated. Some of the old-timers believe that it was better — life was easier in those days. But then there was alcohol.

The Indian had never discovered the art of making intoxicating drinks, though the Hurons did make a thin, sour gruel from corn that had been allowed to ferment.

It is rather interesting to note that at a very early period, before the liquor was introduced in the prairies, the Blackfeet Indians had no interest in drinking at all. When liquor

90

was first introduced, it was given out free to the Indians to induce them to come to trade. In the beginning the Blackfeet wouldn't even accept the liquor; they didn't want it, and it was only through the fact that the Hudson Bay and other companies almost forced the Indians to take it, as a means of getting control over them, that they finally accepted liquor. In the Blackfoot language, liquor is known as *Nabiochi*, which means white man's water.

In 1811 the diary of a trader gives us this picture:

> To see a houseful of drunken Indians consisting of men, women, and children is a most unpleasant sight. For in that condition they often wrangle, pull each other by the hair and fight. At some time ten or twelve of both sexes may be seen fighting each other promiscuously until at last they all fall on the floor, one upon the other. Some spilling rum out of a small kettle or dish which they hold in the hand, while others are throwing up that which they've just drunk. To add to this uproar, a number of children, some on their mother's shoulders and others running about and taking hold of their clothes and constantly bawling, the older ones through fear that their parents may be stabbed or that some other misfortune may befall them in the fray.
>
> These shrieks of the children form a very unpleasant chorus to the brutal noise kept up by their drunken parents who are engaged in the squabble.

I don't know that this is any different from drunken white families. However, excessive use of alcohol was the start of the trouble that has been plaguing my people ever since the first coming of the white man. There are areas of the country where drinking is an extremely big problem.

The following were the more obvious results of the white man's influence: drunkenness, disease, war, the declining population, starvation in some areas after the white man joined in hunting the buffalo. But something else began to happen; as the white man and his culture spread

91

westward, so did the decay of the native arts. First the Indian lost his native arts, as he turned to the white man's modern ways; then the government took a hand.

After the white men came, and especially after they put the Indian on the reservation, the wisdom of the old men in governing their tribal affairs was substituted by putting in the Indian agents. The religion introduced was quite at variance with the religious rituals of the Indian people themselves. In fact, Indian religion was frowned upon, and perhaps even laughed away as being superstition and as coming from the devil rather than from a beneficent Great Spirit in which all Indian tribes believe. I have always felt that so sensitive is the primitive mind, which is almost childlike in its belief, that if you destroy one part of their society, the rest tends to crumble and deteriorate.

The whole attitude of the white man towards the Indian seemed to become one of contempt. This, however, wasn't so true of the farmers and trappers, who knew their Indian friends better. But the merchants and the army authorities and the government agents certainly gave the Indians the feeling that they were looked down on.

In olden days the agent never had respect for my people. They used to go to the agent's door, and most of the time he would slam the door in their faces. And, even if an Indian child were sick, he couldn't be taken to the hospital in town. The sick had to be looked after in some kind of a house on the reservation. Many children were lost just through carelessness, not getting the right medical attention. But since, you must try to understand, my people tried to live differently and to have no hatred for white people.

It seems as if our native cultures were being deliberately broken down. The Indian agents often knew little about us and cared less. It meant little to them that the old man knocking at their door might be a hereditary chief, whose ancestry could be traced back twenty generations, that the chief might have titles and honors, and crests and songs in

92

his name. It became a matter of government policy to civilize Indians by outlawing their pagan religions, their ceremonies, their songs. Even our languages were discouraged on most reservations.

In some places, my people were not permitted to speak in their language at all, at any time during their stay in school. There are some old Indians still living today who paid what they thought in these days was the extreme penalty. They were forbidden to speak in their own language. If they were caught the first time, they were reprimanded severely. If they were caught speaking in their own language the second time, they were, what they called in those days, strapped. They were whipped, and if they were caught the third time, they took their only holidays away from them. That did a great deal of harm. One of the most severe Christian supressors that came, came with the church. The Christians meant well, but they would have done better if they had asked the Indian "What does it all mean?" They might have asked, for instance, "Do you believe in a god?" They would have learned that my people did pray to a specified god. I'm absolutely certain that it's the same god that was taught to my people later on. Had the church asked us this, we would not have gone down so low prior to coming up again. In the process they had a great deal to do with killing our very spirit, with wrenching from our very lives the incentive to be ourselves.

This sounds very critical of the mission schools and of the church's influence in general. You'll hear considerably more criticism from the Indians too. You'll hear how the Indians were encouraged to destroy their totem poles by ignorant missionaries who thought they were pagan symbols. However, you will also hear that the only contact with the white man's world in some remote areas was through the selfless work of the missionary, and the only schools; the only medical attention was provided by the missions. How many Indians who have become nurses and doctors and teachers owe their success to the missions?

93

Naturally speaking, the first milieu or the first surroundings for education are the home. The parents have to be the first educators in the process of bringing up their children. We know that there are many circumstances, there are many situations where the parents cannot or do not have the facilities to take this responsibility over their children. They want them to be educated, but they do not know how. So they take their child to a boarding school because they want them to learn, they want them to be educated. This is the purpose of boarding schools. The segregated school is where all Indian children are together, learning together, living together. The children are in a place where the teachers and the supervisors, because of their experience, because of their understanding, will be able to help the children with their education, help them to further understand themselves and give them the help that their parents cannot.

I've been pretty critical of the white man and the effect he's had on us since he arrived in our country. However, we should look on the other side of the picture too.

At the turn of the century, the Indian population had declined to approximately 130,000 in Canada and 260,000 in the United States. The incidence of tuberculosis was extremely high. About one out of five families had a relative or a member suffering either advanced tuberculosis, or incipient tuberculosis. With the change in the thinking on government administration, a program of health and medical care — by no means as advanced as private programs — was instituted, which has been really remarkable insofar as cutting down the incidence of disease and death among my people; so that today, we have a population of nearly 200,000 in Canada and over 700,000 in the United States. This is one of the highest birth increases of any of the ethnic groups in Canada. It is largely due to better health conditions and better food for the Indians. There's no doubt about it that the relief and welfare program of the government has done much to keep away starvation. However, this has not done the work of giving them that background of good nutrition that makes them good workers.

You must not forget the white people have had centuries of civilization, if you may call it civilization, as a background. But my people do not have much more than a hundred years or so of white man's culture. However, my people had their own culture, their own way of thinking, their own way of living; and then all at once the white man came with his ideas, his culture, and pushed the Indians onto reservations — pieces of land where my people are gathered together, where they are secluded from the white man. At first the white men were afraid of the Indians and the Indians were afraid of the white men. Then the Indians developed a tribal attitude. The white people developed their own attitude. So much so, that for quite a while they would not mix. Now all at once the white man wants to know — "Why don't they mix?" "Why should we not mix them together?" This is something that has to be well understood by both parties, by the whites, as well as by the Indians. If they have a common understanding, then they will realize it themselves. Why should we not help one another as true brothers?

Termination of the long-established relations between the federal government and my people should occur only after there is adequate information before the federal government, the Indians, the local people and their governments as to what will happen to all four parties involved if the tribe is terminated. This requires the solution of legal, governmental, financial, and human problems. Adequate time must be allowed for the Indians, their neighbors, state and local units and all others who might be affected by the change to work out the necessary adjustments.

My people should be allowed full hearings before the appropriate congressional committees.

95

The government's responsibility should be relinquished only when the Indians are no longer in the lower segment of our culture in education, health, and economic status. The tribesmen must also be qualified and willing to take on the additional responsibilities, and be ready to take advantage of the wider social, economic, and political benefits, on a comparable basis with their neighbors and without discrimination.

In order that Indians may be able to make their own decisions, cooperate in the execution of a plan, and take responsibility for the results, they should participate fully at every turn. The participation should consist in working out the procedure from its earliest stages and continuing with the discussions during the maturing of the program, as well as in voting for or against the final formulation. The process should involve not only leaders but the tribesmen as well. Testing should determine to what extent the people affected actually know what is being planned or presented. The freedom of Indians to accept or reject a program should not be tied to offers of payment from federally held tribal funds, or, in the case of favorable action, to offers of later payment.

Ordinarily, any per capita or other payments should be distributed in small sums over a period of time so that there is an opportunity for the recipients to learn how to handle cash before all assets are dissipated.

Final decisions affecting programs should be preceded by plans acceptable to the tribe for managing, utilizing, or dividing tribal properties. To this end, Indians should have competent and skilled assistance, paid for when necessary by the United States. The desirability and probable consequences of each plan should be discussed in advance and thoroughly understood by the Indians, the other people of the area, and the state and local officials.

The legislation should expressly recognize that the Indian rights do not derive from the state but exist independently of state law. Legislation should ensure the federal courts exclusive jurisdiction over any lawsuit arising, as long as the land remains in Indian ownership.

However, the younger generation today is living a lot better than did our ancestors. That is, they have a chance of making a good living.

There is more money now. They have better things, better houses. However, their manners are not as good as the old Indians; they are losing their Indianness, if you will.

Yes, more money, better houses, better health, the secluded life, no responsibility. Certainly things are better than they were. Many on the reservations have cars instead of horses. The girls particularly can be very smartly dressed. There is a price to pay for this type of security. The Chief Joseph-Sitting Bull trait seems to be waning — in too many cases it's gone!

This is one of the problems that the public must face up to. A program must be initiated and must be sold. There are two lots of people to sell it to. The government, who wants to control everything, and then the Indians, who live on the reservations, who often think that the government should not change its policies. After a few generations of this false security on the reservation and government control, most of my people on the reservation level don't have the ambition and the initiative they had of old. Therefore, it is understandable that the Indian Service gets bitter sometimes. Furthermore, my people must realize that the Indian Service is made up of human beings.

A lot of my people would never accept this. These people have families, a lot of them have family trouble, sick children. They're under tremendous pressure and they try. It's pretty difficult to please everybody. They're in a position where they have to keep everybody happy, their bosses in Ottawa and Washington — and the unrelenting pressures of public opinion.

Therefore, understanding the needs of my people is of

tremendous importance when attempting to alter their world. That is why education should be the focus of all government policy affecting my people. We must restore the Indian's pride of origin and faith in themselves, a faith which was undermined by years of political and economic suppression by the federal government. We must arouse a desire in them to share the benefits of modern civilization. These are deeply human considerations. If neglected, they will defeat the best-intentioned government plans.

As a result, too many Indians who have already entered the dominant society have generally disdained their historic background, drawing away from it as though ashamed. Instead of serving as a bridge to enable others to move freely between the two worlds, they have too often interpreted their heritage imperfectly to the majority race and have proved powerless in explaining their adopted culture to their own people.

No program imposed from above can serve as a substitute for one willed by Indians themselves. Mere consent to a plan is not sufficient. Such "consent" may be passive, representing a submission to the inevitable; or it may be obtained without their full understanding, before they are either able or willing to shoulder unfamiliar responsibilities; or actually may be opposition. What is essential is to elicit their own initiative and intelligent cooperation.

While emphasis should as hitherto be put on fitting Indian youth for its new opportunities and responsibilities, we must not divorce them from the old Indian culture. In their society and in their religion, Indians believe they have values worth preserving. These are sometimes stated in mystical terms, and if related to the Supreme Being, are sometimes kept secret. Nonetheless they exist. Two examples out of many involve their idea of unity and their reverence for Mother Earth.

Unity is demonstrated by the Indians' willingness to work with others and do their part. They give their strength and help to perpetuate the traditional culture. Cohesion is also furthered in many tribes by a veneration for elders and reliance on their wisdom. Status and personal security is often gained by service. Sinking oneself into the group tends to discourage competitiveness or a pride in the possession of materials objects for their monetary value. This attitude is perhaps one reason for the improvidence of many Indians. Since ideals, however, are not consistently achieved, exceptions to the norm are found in every group.

The spiritual attachment to nature, an essential aspect of many pre-Columbian cultures, has brought the Indian into an intimate accord with the elements. This appears strikingly evident in my people's attitude toward land. Land is believed to be part of a benevolent mother and, like her, vital to life. Among Indian tribes it was generally considered to be not a merchantable product but one the user had the natural right to enjoy. These attitudes and the attachment of their ancient religion and customs still tend to persist. This is one reason that termination or liquidation of Indian lands must be very carefully considered. What has kept him alive undoubtedly was the fact that he could identify himself with a portion of Mother Earth.

These and related ideas, if given due weight as part of the Indian's heritage, will prevent the confusion brought about in both races by the assumption that assimilation may be achieved through Indians' adopting a few simple attitudes of their white neighbors. For example, it is often said that the Indian needs to be thrifty, to acquire habits of diligence, and to learn the importance of punctuality.

Yet in their own culture, where the goals were understood, Indians were economical, were hard-working, and possessed a keen appreciation of time. Thrift was shown in their utilization of every part of animals killed in the chase, as well as by their gathering and drying of berries and edible roots. Hunting or tilling the soil with wooden sticks to grow enough food for the family demanded a high

99

order of perseverance. The element of time for the agriculturists was determined by the planting and harvesting seasons, and for the hunter by the habits of the animals he stalked down. In each case, time was a vital factor, though not in the white man's sense of hours and minutes marked on the clock. His clock was the sun.

In occupations which appeal to the established Indian ideals, such as those calling for facing danger, for careful craftsmanship, or for common effort, Indians have not only found satisfaction but have achieved national recognition. Teams of Iroquois are outstanding structural steelworkers on high bridges and skyscrapers; groups of Apache, Blackfoot, Shoshone, and Pueblo "Red-Hats," flown to fight fires in the western forests, have excelled at this perilous work; and the demand for Navajos in factories which require delicate precision work is well known.

Nor should it be overlooked that Indian values are not unique. "Honor thy father and thy mother" is a commandment found among many peoples. The importance of any set of values does not arise from their origin, existence, uniqueness, or validity. What is of concern is that we recognize those values of the Indian in making plans for the race.

So-called government assistance also requires a new look. Since 1933 the white man's society has been meeting its human needs in ways similar to those traditional to Indian tribes. "Sharing" was, with them, a means of helping the helpless. The United States has supplied comparable relief through social security, an aid to the old, the blind, the dependent, crippled children, and the unemployed, as well as by free distribution of surplus commodities. In other respects also, it has been extending to the entire population the kind of help formerly given only to Indians. Such things as federal financial assistance for public schools, scholarships, the construction of highways and hospitals, and medical aid to the elderly are now benefits available to or planned for all Americans. These services have come

100

as a consequence of acts of Congress. The Indians through the years have received theirs as the result of bargains set forth in treaties, agreements, statutes, and policies.

As the outlook of two civilizations converges and the services to the rest of the people, financed partially or largely by the United States, actually outstrip those once given only to Indians, the movement of Indians into the broader society will be facilitated. What the members of this underprivileged race need is more and better education, improved economic assistance, a better state of health, and a more carefully designed preparation for the responsibilities of the white man's way of life. Provided that they can avail themselves of the services enjoyed by the rest of society and also that they find material opportunities appropriate to their abilities, Indians must receive comparable benefits from government social services.

Indian policy must motivate the Indian individual, the Indian family, and the Indian community to participate in solving their own problems. The Indian must be given responsibility, must be afforded an opportunity he can use, and must develop faith in himself.

Indian-made plans, when workable, should be adopted.

Government policy must stimulate education, health, and economic development. To be effective, it must have a deep regard of Indian heritage, which is important not only to the Indians but also the cultural enrichment of America. It has been said that on this continent the American Indian culture is a giant pearl in a bank of sand. And the institution of the League of the Iroquois in a modern and larger cloak girdles the globe as a savior of this civilization.

Even before the league, my people were leaders of civilization. While the Roman Empire fell and Europe passed into the dark ages, the Mayas (of modern Yucatán, Guatemala, and Honduras) built a great civilization. From the fourth to the sixteenth centuries their city-like centers thrived in the lush rain land and rivaled ancient Greece.

101

Directed by an enlightened nobility, Maya artisans and craftsmen constructed giant public buildings. Between one thousand and two thousand years before Pope Gregory XIII (in 1582) invented today's calendar, Mayan philosophers and mathematicians were using a more accurate system. A thousand years before the Hindus, the American Indian conceived of the zero. My ancestors also worked out the revolutions of the moon, the length of the Venusian year, and the recurrence of the solar eclipses.

Treaty Makers

An important and far-reaching effect of the white man's contact with the Indian is bound up with the treaties. One of the first treaties was made by the French in 1680.

Yes, the Indian country has been changing ever since the white man first started taking over. However, its present path was set when my people signed the treaties, most of them a little more than a hundred years ago, but some as early as the seventeenth century.

A lot has been said by both Indians and non-Indians about the iniquities of these treaties: about the way the invaders took advantage of the Indian's simplicity, and the way the government's obligations haven't been lived up to. Perhaps we should first understand the spirit of the times, the limited nature of the Indian's needs, and the flowery pomposity of the white race in the early days of colonization and expansion.

Your great white father in Washington or the Queen Mother across the ocean (in Canada) wishes the good of

103

all races under his sway. He wishes his red children to be happy and contented. He wishes them to live in comfort; he wishes order and peace to reign through all his country. And while his arm is strong to punish the wicked man, his hand is also open to reward the good man everywhere in his dominion.

Long before Queen Victoria and the government in Washington, the early French settlers had made treaties. In 1680, Louis, by the grace of God, King of France and of Navarre formally recognized the rights of Indians in Quebec. Then in 1763, King George the Third issued a royal proclamation which provided that no Indian could be dispossessed of his lands without both his own consent and the consent of the crown. This meant in effect that Indian title to the land was recognized and could be extinguished only by agreement with the Indians and then only to the crown. This is what led to the series of formal agreements that came to be known as the Indian treaties. The first treaty signed by the Canadian government is dated September 7, 1850 and the latest is as recent as 1923. In the United States the first treaty was signed in 1790. It was with the Creek Indians of the southeast. This treaty was a great accomplishment for the new republic as it assured the peace and safety of the southern border against the Spanish, then in Louisiana and Florida. The Creek nation ceded lands north of the thirty-first parallel. And, in turn, the United States guaranteed the remaining boundaries of the Creek nation, some 84,000 square miles.

However, you cannot say that the introduction of the fashion, the white man cast covetous eyes on that land. In 1791, the Secretary of War sent an Indian agent through the territory of the Creeks (Georgia). He reported that it "must, in the process of time, become a most delectable part of the United States."

In 1871 the United States discontinued the practice of treaty negotiation with Indian tribes. Thus came to an end the era of forked-tongue diplomacy — some 386 treaties had been written.

The treaties generally went like this: "What I offer you is to be while the water flows and the sun rises. The government will agree to give two hoes, one spade, one scythe and one axe for every family actually settled; one plough for every ten families, five harrows for every twenty families and a yoke of oxen, a bull and four cows for every band, and enough barley, wheat and oats to plant the land they've actually broken up."

The treaties promised all sorts of things to the Indian. The main thing that the Indian gave up was claims to the lands that he ceded to the government. What does that mean? It would seem reasonable that all the land not ceded to the government belongs to the Indians still. That is where there's still a lot of disagreement. In British Columbia, there's never been a treaty. The Indians never ceded any land to the Crown. Therefore, who owns British Columbia today?

What exactly is a treaty? It's a legal document signed by both parties in agreement. Usually it was the lieutenant governor, a general, or the Indian commissioner who signed on behalf of the government. One or more of the chiefs of the assembled bands signed on behalf of the Indians. The usual procedure was to call a meeting of all the chiefs and important members of the bands concerned, explain the purpose of the meeting, and state the wishes of the governor. There would be hours and often days of discussion and debate. Sometimes whole bands would attend. When this happened, the problem of feeding these large assemblies for days on end became acute. The wise old chiefs bargained well with an eye to the future. Published transcripts of the proceedings read like this:

"I ask you a question. In years to come we shall see things that run swiftly, that go by fire, carriages and we ask you that us Indians may not have to pay their passage on these things but can go free."

105

"I think the best thing that I can do is to become an Indian. I cannot promise them a pass on the railway free."

"We must have the privilege of traveling about the country where it is vacant."

"Of course, I told them so."

"Should we discover any metal that was of use, could we have the privilege of putting our own price on it?"

"If any important minerals are discovered on any of their reservations, the minerals will be sold for their benefit."

When the treaty was finally signed, the government had agreed to make various concessions to the Indians, in exchange for all rights to the land the Indians had lived on for centuries. Most of us nowadays know pretty well what our rights are, but you'd wonder how our ancestors ever made sense out of any treaty.

For example: "Whereas the Indians inhabiting the said country have been notified and informed by her Majesty's commissioners that it is the desire of her Majesty to open up for settlement a tract of country hereinafter described. The tract embracing an area of fifty-five-thousand square miles."

This agreement is typical of the thirteen principal treaties and it covers, among other things, reservations of one square mile per family of five. The government had the right to sell or lease reservation lands with the consent of the Indians and to appropriate lands for federal public purposes, subject to the compensation. The Indians would be provided with schools and have the right to hunt, trap, and fish on lands surrendered subject to government regulations. There would be control of liquor, provision of an annual grant for ammunition, and twine for nets. An annual payment of twelve dollars would be made to each person, twenty-five dollars to each chief, fifteen dollars to each headman, a suit of clothes every three years for chiefs and headmen.

My people, affected citizens, and the government are

still arguing about treaty rights to this day. Did the Indian get a fair return for all his land, or has he been gypped? And you'll still hear Indians complaining about the government agents not living up to their promises. The old chiefs had a long list of demands. They don't seem very important today, but they were important to the Indians then. There was not much they asked for that wasn't granted.

In other treaties, the chiefs asked for ammunition, twine for making nets, crosscut saw, a whip saw, a grindstone, files, exemption from military services, an interpreter, and free meals at all meetings.

Was the Indian satisfied with what he got? Did he really understand what he was signing? All the indications are that he was satisfied. And he wasn't tricked into signing. However, I doubt very much if my people understood the real significance of the Indian treaties.

They usually took some time to deliberate over the provisions of the treaty and asked occasionally to have certain passages explained — more especially those in relation to the reservation. Before signing it, they presumably comprehended the nature of the obligation into which they were about to enter. That the surrender of their territorial rights would be irrevocable. That they were to stand forever afterwards in new relation to the white man.

I think if I were a chief at that time, I should have regretted the passing of the old days. But I think I'd have foreseen that it had to be — and so long as we kept enough land for ourselves, we might as well get whatever help and protection we could from the white man. I don't think I could have looked ahead far enough to see that the twelve dollars a year would hardly be worth getting in the 1970s, or ten dollars or five dollars, which is about what some of the bands settled for. Three hundred pounds of tobacco seemed a lot then. So did a new suit of clothes. At that time, my people wanted to be left in peace on the parcels of land they had been assigned, but since then things have changed. I doubt if either side, the government or the Indians, could have foreseen that Indians would one day be in the government, or be doctors and lawyers, senators, schoolteachers. In a sense, the treaties of long ago were good for the people at that time. However, now we have advanced beyond the age of the oxen.

The Indian is a very trusting fellow. Instead of putting something down in black and white, he horse-traded a deal by word of mouth. Indians by nature are easy going. At the time the treaties were written, the white man and the Indian probably acted in good faith. Both sides tried to abide by the treaties, but the times, the people, the governments changed. There were a lot of treaties. They wrote treaties for all occasions.

Some treaties state that the government will take care of my people, teach them how to make a living just like the white man; which they haven't done in most cases.

My people are just now taking advantage of education, but it will take a few years before that education can bear fruit. You take the reservation potential. Look at the wealth that has been produced from a similar piece of ground, adjacent to the reservation. Why shouldn't the reservation produce the same? Why couldn't there have been development? There should be expert businessmen supervising it in order for the reservation Indians to pay their own way. The Indians should have been induced to settle down, the same as the rest of the community. If it weren't for the treaties, what would have become of us? However, we have the treaties, we have a little piece of land which belongs to the Indian.

At least the treaties give my people a home and a living. Before the treaties, the disappearance of the buffalo had reduced the people of the Plains to starvation. Some tribes, for instance, were eating mice and dogs and old buffalo skins to keep alive. And you could have seen a dignified old chief sitting at a gopher hole, with a snare, trying to catch himself a meal. It was the reservations and the treaties that saved the Indians from extinction in many areas.

Not all the Indians are really under treaty. Some of the nontreaty Indians get the same rights and privileges as do the Indians under treaties. However, in Canada more than twenty-five-thousand halfbreeds or metis are not included. In the United States the nonreservation Indians are excluded. Anyway, good or bad, right or wrong, the treaties were signed. The Indian lived up to his part of the bargain and the white man must live up to his. An act to regulate dealing with Indian service in Canada was drawn up in 1876 and completely overhauled in 1951. And it's this present Indian Act which is responsible for ensuring the Indian's rights as well as their restrictions through the Indian Affairs Branch of the Department of Citizenship and Immigration. The Indians were promised schools. Under the act they can be educated either in special Indian schools or in white schools — and the university education is paid for, though the sad state of learning of the older generation today supports the Indian charges of bad schools, poor teachers, and muddled administration in the past.

The Indians were promised a medicine chest; the act provides for free medical care, though the Indian will tell you the free medicine is of little use on an isolated reserve, fifty miles from the nearest doctor. They were promised exemption from taxation, protection against alcohol. They are still free of taxes while they are on the reserves but liquor restrictions are being relaxed, at the request of the individual bands. What they weren't promised was a government agent or superintendent on every reservation, government control over every decision of their councils, over their land deals, over their lives; a control that many Indians claim has sapped their spirit and killed their initiative.

I think that Indians all over the country will agree that the Indian Act and the Bureau of Indian Affairs were designed to protect us, but have now put us in the state of protective custody. However, the opposite was intended.

The Indian is a full citizen, yet he's restricted in what he does and how he does it. What's the answer to it all? This is a big question. Take the Bill of Rights for instance. Are we going to have a dual legal standard throughout the Indian country — a Bill of Rights for all the general population and another act for the Indians? Should we have a separate set of laws for an Indian that's far advanced, another for an Indian that's not quite so far advanced as, say the Indians of this or that district, as the Indians of the north? After all, we have Indians who are doctors and lawyers, who are prominent in the big cities.

I feel that there is a need for changes. Too many people, charged with the responsibility for Indian welfare, know nothing about what goes on at the reservation level.

Here is another common complaint. A few resolutions are passed by the tribal business council, then sent on to the government agencies for approval. After much delay, the resolution is returned from the central office wih an emphatic "No!" attached. However, the Indians think it is all right — there seems to be a sort of a fatalism about the operation of a tribal business council. They don't really expect anything.

Perhaps we need an organization of Indians from each reservation to serve as consultants. They would know the conditions on the reservations. Better yet, we should have Indian superintendents and agents. I believe it would be a good thing to have some kind of an Indian Advisory Committee, especially if the provinces and the states take over the reservations; which might be soon coming about.

The Indian should get out and support himself. The white man has failed for one reason or another. However, this failure has constantly been a detriment to the Indians, and not to the white man.

The treaties, instead of helping the Indians, have worked a hardship on him. However, the treaties did save my people from extinction. In Canada, the Indian Act discriminates against the Indian, and contravenes the Bill of Rights, or, as the courts have ruled it, takes precedence. Should the Indian continue to get treaty money and a protected life? Or should we throw away all the Indian legislation and let him take his chance in the white man's world?

Indian Culture

Life of the Indian, like the way of the white man, has its foundations in the cultures and traditions of our race. It has not been long since our art, our religion, our songs and dances, and all the traditions that make a people different from the rest of the world, were flourishing without any outside influence. But when the white man came, the winds of change began to blow.

The word *culture* means many things to many people. Some of us immediately think of Shakespeare, of classical music, and Latin and Greek. But the Indian peoples were rich in culture without even having a written language of their own. Their languages, two thousand of them recorded on the American continents, were part of their culture. Their stories, their legends, their beliefs in the origins of their people, and their land were part of their culture.

Here is a typical old-time Indian story: In the early days, when the world was very young, Coyote, the Creator, found himself alone and lonely. There was nothing but water

112

everywhere, and the air above it, of course. To relieve his loneliness, he created Beaver, Muskrat, and Otter, but he soon grew tired of them. The real trouble he decided, was the water. "It's not solid enough," he said to himself. "I want something I can rest my feet on. I believe that if I could stand on something solid, I could put one foot in front of the other and walk about." Suddenly the answer came to him. Under the water, of course! There must be something solid there. So he tied his longest fishing line to the Muskrat and told him to dive as deep as he could and try to bring something up from the bottom of the water. The Muskrat was gone a long, long time, and came up at last so faint and weary that he died. But between his paws was a little ball of mud. Coyote took this and rolled it in his hands, and as he did so it grew larger and larger and larger. He kneaded it and molded it until at last he had a huge ball of mud so big that thousands of people and animals could live on it. There was room for trees to grow and rivers to flow. But because Coyote had been in such a hurry, there were big stretches of wet land that we call muskeg, and these never will be dry. This is an animal story — similar stories abound in the Indian country. The popularity of animal stories today can be seen in Walt Disney's success (he must have gotten some of his ideas from Indian stories).

Culture is the way of living adopted by any specific group of people. It embraces their clothes, their tools and weapons, food, languages, religion, art, social organization, transportation; everything, in fact, that is a part of their way of living.

The culture of the Indians was by no means the same from coast to coast. Some tribes were extremely primitive, with almost no social organization except the family group. Others, such as the Iroquois and certain West Coast tribes, southeastern, and eastern tribes were highly organized. Although the culture of a particular race enriched the

113

lives of those particular people, there is little doubt that those racial characteristics should be shared and adapted by others.

The Indian characteristic has much to add to enriching the national spirit of both Canada and the United States. This is something that has been completely neglected. I have spoken to Indian groups of assorted sizes and from different tribes. Most of them have not the foggiest idea of the proud lineage of tradition that they have in the Indian race. They forget that the Indian was responsible for the development of corn and the potato. Every time we smoke a cigarette we are burning incense to the skill of some ancient Indian agriculturalist. This is a matter of pride, just as the Scot is proud of his kilt and his tartan. His proud boast is, "That where MacGregor sits is the head of the table." This is what should be rejuvenated in my people.

It was among the more advanced people, those who lived in semipermanent villages and had an assured food supply, that the arts and sciences began to develop. The southern and northeastern and the West Coast people perfected one of the most highly sophisticated art forms ever seen. The Iroquois had advanced forms of government long before white influence began to be felt. Remnants of the old Indian cultures are still numerous, some of them quite strong. It will probably be many years before the last vestige disappears, especially in religion and in mental attitudes. Among the Iroquois, their pre-Christian, Long House religion is still followed by a large number of people. There was a simplicity and a personal appeal about the old religions that many Indians still remember with affection.

To many of the old-timers, there is too much conflict between religions. The old way, when they had just one Creator, was simple to them. It didn't matter how many different Indian tribes there were in North America, there was the one Creator. But now there are so many different concepts of the divine, or the lack of one, that it seems in this regard civilization is regressing. Perhaps my people should continue to approach their God in the manner of our ancestors. They should continue to make pilgrimages to the mountaintops or to the bathing pools or to the external sweat house to take a sweat bath.

Whatever they called their God — the Creator, Nature, the Great Spirit, the Maker of Life — theirs wasn't the pagan religion the white man's government and the church considered it to be. They even outlawed the Sun Dance, a dance that was done all across the plains. This was the Sun Dance of the stony Indians and the Blood Blackfeet. However, there's one thing about the Indian: if he's religious at all, he really enjoys going to church and singing hymns.

Even among the Indians who we look upon as very much integrated in the white way of life, there are those who profess to be Christians and yet attend secret spirit dances. The dancing season is in the winter. Every reservation, from north to south and from east to west, has a big smokehouse or dancehouse. These hold hundreds of people. The people gather from long distances, from several different tribes. They're seated in their special places. After the dancing starts, the dancers dance one at a time, each dancer in turn becomes possessed with his Guardian Spirit. This is rather a strange thing to see and hear, because when it starts he begins to sob and cry out. This loud sobbing sounds like he is crying, then it turns into a song. At that point others pick up the song with their drums and sticks, with which they are beating time. They sing his song for him several times over. Then he gets up and dances around the fire or pole in the center of the room. These affairs have lasted from five in the afternoon right through the night until daylight in the morning. Not everybody can be chosen to be a singer or a dancer. You can't volunteer. A dancer or singer must be chosen and then initiated. The initiation takes four days with special ceremonies every morning and every evening. Although they wouldn't admit it, they don't

115

think of this as religion. However, white people think that they actually get a religious experience out of this contact with some supernatural force that possesses them. Just because some religious groups go around beating on drums, blowing horns, and singing, that is not sufficient evidence to term Indian ceremonies as religious. Furthermore, so-called experts should stop trying to compare our Indian culture on their limited scale, their limited frame of reference. "Sing along with Mitch" could be called religion by the standards of some anthropologists.

What they are expressing when they are out there dancing on the floor is, "I'm an Indian and I'm proud of it." In many other parts of the Indian country old ceremonies are still performed.

There is the Rain Dance. This usually takes place in the spring of the year, or, say, after the leaves come on; that's when they make the Rain Dance. It lasts three days and three nights. It has been carried on for years and years. It has been a custom that my people have always believed in. More times than not they have succeeded.

But not all the dances have a purely religious significance. The Indians love to dance, and in some areas never a week goes by without the the resounding of the drums to the chicken dances. This is part of our customs. My people like to dance. There used to be different societies. Today the white man has many different clubs. However, the old secret societies have died; but the chicken dance, grass dance, owl dance, and the round dance are still being performed.

Indian languages are fading away. These languages are difficult to learn. Mostly my people talk English. Eventually the Indian languages will die.

As for the written language, none of the Indians north of Mexico had the art of writing. True, they could draw and paint pictures from which some meaning can be derived, but there was not an alphabet or a system of recording words or thoughts. However, missionaries did

116

devise various systems whereby it was possible to write Indian languages, the best known being the syllabics devised by the Rev. James Evans about 1840.

Undoubtedly you have heard about *wampum* as a means of recording stories and events. Wampum was the white man's abbreviation of the longer Indian word *wampampiak*, meaning approximately, "a string of white shells." It consisted of cylindrical beads, about a third of an inch long, and an eighth of an inch in diameter. Wampum, when strung together with sinew thread, was used as money by both Indians and the early white settlers. The beads were also used to make belts, which were used to remind the parties of a treaty or the terms of a certain treaty. The wampum belts could not be read, as we read a book, but were merely memory joggers. Thus a belt might have woven into it a dark man, in purple beads, and a white man, in white beads. Connecting these two would be a line of beads, either purple or white, signifying the mutual understanding between them.

Artistic expression took different forms in different parts of the Indian country. On the plains, geometrical designs, stylized with lively, realistic figures, were beaded and painted on leather. In eastern Canada, floral patterns were common. On the West Coast and in the Southwest art was more fully developed than anywhere else. The abstract designs on flat surfaces such as the sides of wooden chests and pottery, while based originally on animal forms, are so stylized as to be at times unrecognizable. The carving of masks and totem poles, rattles and the handles of horn spoons are extremely skillful. Totem poles, incidentally, reached their flourish and climax after the introduction of steel tools by the whites. In the Southwest, the Indian artists developed great skill in pottery and metal work.

Personal names were important to the Indian. Names were often changed at important stages in a man's life. The names were beautiful and colorful for the most part,

117

and are used to this day — Eagletail, Heavenfire, Coming Daylight, Wandering Spirit, Flying Strawberry, Crooked Legs, Day Walker, Melting Tallow, Holy White Man, Shot on Both Sides. All have their origins in the Indian culture, like the lady called Born with Tooth, Whose Child Was Born Recently with Two Teeth. And Poking Fire, a connection with the firekeeper of the Longhouse tradition.

Indian songs and legends, too, were a part of our history. There was a song for every occasion; like the Iroquois song for taking the kettle off the fire, or the Yakima song for picking berries.

My people's story would never be complete without mention of the famous potlatch ceremony of the West Coast, a ceremony performed on many important occasions. It was also a form of insurance, which worked roughly like this: A man, to increase his social standing and prestige, would seize on some appropriate occasion to give a potlatch. The name itself, *potlatch*, comes from the Nootka Indian language, meaning "to give." At the potlatch, the man who did the giving would give away a large amount of valuables, such as canoes, oolachen oil, or slaves in the old days. The greater his wealth, the greater was his generosity and the more determined his efforts to give certain men, his rivals in social status, more than they could afford to accept. For it was the rival's duty, when they in their turn gave a potlatch, to return to the first man his gift along with as much as a hundred percent interest. Unfortunately, the displays of ostentatious waste, such as the burning of canoes and oolachen oil, and the killing of slaves, became so flagrant as to force the government to prohibit the potlatch. There was also special potlatch music.

Social organization at times was most complex. The people were classified in order of prestige. At the top, there was a a small group of wealthy and influential men comparable to the nobles of feudal England. Below these men were the men of slightly lesser importance, but who were

118

still a privileged class and who could rise into the rank of the nobles when sufficiently rich, by marriage, or for some outstanding merit. Below these two upper classes were the common people, free, but not of the aristocracy which was barred to them except in the most exceptional cases. Lowest of all were the slaves, of whom there were many hundreds at the time the white man first arrived. They were not ill-treated, but shared the usual occupations of other men in the village. Nevertheless, their lives were at the disposal of their masters, and one or more slaves might be buried under the main post of a new house, or used as rollers for the launching of a new and important canoe. Naturally, this system broke down completely under the pressure of white culture.

There are many forms of Indian culture. Just as in any other culture, legend plays an important part; but it is not always accurate.

One thing is accurate, however: in the United States, Indian affairs is big business. During the one hundred or more years which have elapsed since the United States Government ceased to make treaties with Indian tribes, Congress has appropriated millions of dollars[1] to finance the Indian Service. Both with and without federal assistance, many Indians have left the reservations and taken up new lives for themselves among their non-Indian neighbors. However, significant numbers have remained in Indian country and preserved their tribal identities.[2]

From time to time during the past century, critics of the federal Indian program have raised the question of how long the government must continue its special relationship with Indians. Underlying their concern has been an awareness of the accelerating cost of the program, a belief that to provide special services for Indians places them in a privileged category, and a contention that, because of excessive paternalism, the federal program prevents Indians from achieving their maximum degree of self-sufficiency.

119

An examination of the history and present status of Indian affairs reveals a certain justification for the reservations which these critics have expressed. Annual direct expenditures by the federal government for its services to Indians have risen from over $7 million in 1871 to more than $160 million in 1961 and nearly $240 million in 1969. Many treaties and hundreds of federal statutes qualify Indians for services in the fields of health, education, welfare, banking and land management, which are not available from governmental sources to any other group of Americans. Furthermore, the administration of these services has often been characterized by a paternalistic emphasis which has fostered continuing Indian dependence.

Beset by criticisms based on pragmatic and philosophical considerations such as those listed above, federal administrators and congressmen have at various times offered proposals for terminating the special relationship between Indians and the federal government. A paramount feature of many of these proposals has been the abolition of the Indian Service. Such demands were strongly made in the last years of the nineteenth century, during the years 1917-1918 and 1922-1924, and have dominated much of the federal Indian policy in recent years.

Yet, even those who are most eager to end this special relationship are troubled by the fact that the bulk of the reservation Indian population is less educated than other Americans, has a shorter life span, and has a much lower standard of living. Furthermore, critics of the present program know that states in which many of these Indians reside have limited financial resources and, unless they are subsidized from the federal treasury, cannot undertake the rehabilitation programs which are necessary if Indians within their jurisdictions are to advance economically, socially, and politically.

The distinct legal status of Indians is a further hindrance to the abolishment of the Indian Service and the

120

withdrawal of the federal government from this field. In many decisions, the United States Supreme Court has upheld Washington's responsibility for helping Indians find solutions to their problems. Treaties and statutes still in effect recognize Indians as partial wards of the federal government and as representatives of "domestic, dependent nations," while also recognizing them as citizens of the United States.

Through the years, the Indians themselves have come to have an ambivalent regard for the federal government. They look to it for aid, but also resent and resist its attempts to undermine their social and cultural identity. Seldom do they perceive any connection between what they want and the demands upon them which securing it imposes. Similarly, many well-intentioned non-Indians who recognize and respect the underlying philosophies of the Indian way of life ignore or fail to see this connection. Thus, while urging Indians on the one hand to retain the old ways, they exhort the federal government to improve Indian health and the Indian standard of living, changes which cannot be provided without affecting the old ways they wish to preserve.

Confronted by conflicting opinions as to what the Indians' place in American society is and should be, we have had Indian policies enunciated by Congress and the executive which, over the past seventy-five years or more, have run the gamut from extreme harshness to extreme paternalism. Inevitably, the results have disappointed both the Indians and those who were sincerely and deeply concerned about Indian welfare.

Even with all its complexities, the job of developing and administering an effective program for American Indians is not impossible. However, it must be a joint effort. Responsibility for the solution of the many problems confronting each tribe and reservation lies not only with the Indian Service, but also with the Congress, with the Indians, with local agencies of government and very importantly, with the American people. Furthermore, this solution cannot be found through a return to the extremes of the past.

Program of development — development of people and development of resources — are necessary. What we are attempting to do for those in the underdeveloped areas of the world, we can and must also do for the Indians here at home. Furthermore, to insure the success of our endeavor, we must solicit the collaboration of those whom we hope to benefit — the Indians themselves. To do otherwise is contrary to the American concept of democracy. Basically, we must not forget that ours is a program which deals with human beings. We must have faith in their abilities to help themselves and be willing to take some risks with them.

Everything in the Indian's life: his status, his reservation, his rights and privileges, and his local government — is governed by the Bureau of Indian Affairs in the United States, and in Canada by the federal Indian Act. The Indian Act was presumably designed originally to confirm his rights under the treaties and to protect him from white exploitation. Most Indians have a copy of the act, though few can understand or interpret its legal phrasing any better than non-Indians can understand their legislation. And quite definitely the Indian Act is legislation particularly for Indians, regardless of the existence of a Bill of Rights nominally designed for all Canadians. The Bill of Rights states that:

> Every law of Canada shall, unless it is expressly declared by an Act of the parliament of Canada that it shall operate notwithstanding the Canadian Bill of Rights, be so construed and applied as not to abrogate, abridge or infringe or to authorize the abrogation, abridgement or infringement of any of the rights or freedoms herein recognized and declared. . . .

However, in Canada recent court decisions have ruled that the Indian is still governed by the Indian Act — such clauses as those restricting his freedom to buy liquor, for instance. Nevertheless, the federal government is attempting to restore to the Indians a greater measure of self-government though not the kind of government they had in earlier times. Most bands elect their chiefs and council for a period of two years. Some of the old-timers would like to see the old system of hereditary, life chief system back.

1 Since 1789, the U.S. Government has appropriated nearly $3 billion for Indian Affairs. The bulk of this amount has been spent since 1871, when the policy of negotiating treaties with Indian tribes was discontinued. (Committe on Interior and Insular Affairs, House Committee Print No. 38, 85th Congress, 2nd Session, 1959, pp. 20 and 21.)

2 In its most recent request for appropriations, the Bureau of Indian Affairs estimates that there are 360,000 Indians still living on reservations and 160,000 living in other areas (Department of the Interior Justifications for Appropriations, Fiscal Year Ending June 30, 1962, Bureau of Indian Affairs, p. 30).

Indian Government

Life in the Indian country depends very much on the way my people are governed. In the old days, there wasn't much need for laws and police. The hereditary chiefs controlled the people in most tribes. The children were taught to respect the chiefs and the elders and listen to what they said. Now life is different. My people are trying to follow the white man's way and the white man's kind of government.

What about the Indians' education, employment, discrimination, integration? On these topics even the Indians aren't in agreement. What of government? Are the Indians like the non-Indians? Are they really full citizens, just like any other minority ethnic group? Does the Bill of Rights really apply to them?

All Indians in Canada belong to one of about fifty tribes speaking fifty different languages. And there may be several thousand Indians in a tribe, scattered over several thousand square miles. Just like white folks, my people like to gather together in communities, in villages. On the West Coast

124

they may be small and compact, remote fishing villages, miles from anywhere. In other places they are spread over hundreds of acres of reservation land. Every one of these little communities, six hundred of them across Canada, is called a band. And most bands have a chief and council, just like the white man's mayor and council.

So, just like the white man, the Indian has two kinds of government: local and federal. Only in the Indian's case, the local band council doesn't have as much authority, or as many responsibilities, as a mayor; and the federal government has more control over the workings of the local Indian council.

Previous to the white man's coming, an Indian had a form of government — he had the chief and the council. A chief usually trained his son, his eldest or his youngest son, depending on the law of that tribe. He trained, from the time of infancy, this particular boy to be a leader. The leaders were well trained. They had their medicine men, witch doctors. The medical profession of today still uses some of their herbs and barks and things of nature. Then my people had their witch doctors. They had a purpose. Today they are called psychiatrists. For the type of world he lived in, they were quite far advanced. But then the white man began to impose his concept of government on my people.

The following was what one councilman related as his experience of the call to tribal government. "I've never run for a council position. I was nominated and elected. There was nobody to run against me the first time. Second time, my dad ran against me. It was on account of I was too much like a white man, I was moving too fast. But I ran against him. I shouldn't have. I got a lot of respect for age, you know. But his views were the direct opposite to mine, so I ran against him. The older element, it's hard to explain. There are a lot of fellows, you know they can criticize and find fault with the present administration,

125

but I never criticize anybody unless I have something better to put in its place."

However, politicians, no matter what race, seem to have the same line. "I've been drafted. . . ." "I'm the people's choice. . . ." "The will of the people. . . ."

Like Canada, the United States has a Bill of Rights, which applies to all of its citizens, and special laws and regulations which apply to Indians only. Like the Canadian Indian, the Indians in the United States have local governments, for the most part called tribal governments.

Tribal governments exercise the right of home rule in local Indian affairs, subject to limitations prescribed by Congress. Like states and municipalities, they are integral parts of the national governmental structure. Their roots lie in international law, in treaties with the United States, and in decisions of the Supreme Court, beginning with Chief Justice John Marshall, who in *Worcester v. Georgia* (1832) recognized them as "distinct, independent, political communities," a doctrine reasserted by the court as recently as 1954 when it declared that the "basic policy of Worcester has remained." Although Congress can abolish a tribal government by law, it has never done so except by treaty, mutual agreement, or plebiscite, though some would contend that the 1954 termination legislation violated this historic policy.

The Indian Reorganization Act (IRA) of 1934 reaffirmed the broad power already vested in the tribes and granted certain new ones to those willing to accept them. One hundred eighty-one groups voted favorably, with fourteen others coming under the law by inaction; almost one hundred of these adopted frames of government (some, like Eastern Cherokees in North Carolina, already had constitutions); and about seventy-five obtained federal corporate charters for conducting their business affairs. The IRA embodied the view that Indian people can best meet the problems of modern life and fully participate in the

126

general society through corporate, tribal, or other joint action. Although the results have been uneven, Indians made substantial advances. Meanwhile, during the same twenty-five years, great strides have occurred in the surrounding society, so the Indians for the most part still have remained comparatively poor, inadequately educated, and in a state of health below average for the whites.

The Department of the Interior deals with approximately two hundred fifty self-governing reservations. Excluded are those in Oklahoma who at the most have shadow governments, and the groups in Alaska whose background differs from that of tribes in other states.

Indians pay out of their own pockets for their governments, which vary widely in activity and effectiveness. In 1959 the Navajo, the largest of the tribes, with an estimated population of 84,500 (over 125,000 in the early 1970s) and superior economic resources, budgeted $20,150,000 for tribal purposes, including capital improvements and work relief. It made use of between 700 and 750 regular and nearly 3,000 occasional employees, exclusive of Indians on tribal public works. In addition, the federal government expended upwards of $26,000,000 on the tribe. By contrast, the Pueblo of Zia in New Mexico, with a population of 334, had no tribal budget at all and no paid employees.

While Indian governments differ in form, they typically operate under a council democratically elected by the tribesmen for a fixed term. It enacts laws, appoints and fixes the duties and salaries of officers and employees, sets the rules of managing the communal property, appropriates the common funds, and negotiates with local, state, and federal authorities. Important economic transactions, such as leases for agriculture, mineral development, and businesses, must be approved by the council and generally also by the Secretary of the Interior.

Most tribal leaders appear to want to retain their governments. They afford a training in the management of tribal property and in community leadership which the members would not obtain in the surrounding society. Properly taken advantage of by the Indians these governments can be one means by which they enter the wider community at responsible levels. But do they?

Factionalism, however, splits some of the governments, while others embrace too small a group to provide adequate financial support. Moreover, many are finding that the increased demands for services and the skyrocketing costs of administration require the drastic curtailment or even the abandonment of tribal self-rule. Since rapid relinquishment could cause losses, hardship, and frustration, the Indians alone should decide on whether to take that step. The Klamath and Menominee terminations evidenced some of the problems. The Menominees found that only the creation of a new county would make their continued existence practicable, and this requires new laws and accommodations by the state of Wisconsin, whose cooperation they were fortunate to obtain. The dangers and difficulties are increased where a reservation extends into two or even three states, instead of only into several counties of a single state.

Neither Congress nor the states may infringe upon the basic civil rights of Indians, for they enjoy the same protection in respect to these governments as all other American citizens. But the federal judiciary has determined that the guarantees of freedom of worship, speech, and the press, the right to assemble and petition the government, and due process do not restrict tribal action. Thus, a United States court has held that the Navajo could enforce tribal legislation prohibiting the possession or use of peyote on the reservation, even though the ban interferred with the observance of a religion (*Native American Church v. The Navajo Tribal Council,* 1960); nor can a deprivation of religious liberty be redressed under the Civil Liberties Act (*Toledo v. Pueblo of Jemez,* 1954). Similarly, the amendments which forbid the United States and the states

128

to deprive any person of life, liberty, or property without due process of law do not apply to a tribe's conduct of criminal trials (*Talton v. Mayes,* 1896). A tribe can also impose a tax without complying with the due-process requirement (*Barta v. Ogala Sioux Tribe,* 1956).

No government of whatever kind should have the authority to infringe upon fundamental civil liberties; government itself must ever be subject to law. Freedom of religion, utterance, and assembly, the right to be protected in one's life, liberty, and property against arbitrary government action and to be immune from double jeopardy and bills of attainder, and the guarantee of a fair trial are not privileges; they are minimum conditions which all Americans should enjoy. For any tribe to override any of them violates the very assumptions on which our free society was established. The absence of these safeguards will, moreover, retard the economic development of reservations, for business concerns are not likely to risk their capital when confronted with the possibility of arbitrary taxation or similar oppressive measures.

Also different from the non-Indian society, tribes are generally exempt from suits in court unless they and Congress consent. In the case of corporate charters granted under IRA, however, court actions are authorized against tribes, with some limitations. This provision should be extended to the unincorporated tribes, for as they seek to develop industries, they are more apt to succeed if they can be sued under conditions which both give industry protection and safeguard the tribe.

My people would be wise to reexamine their government to ascertain to what extent they are still useful. Can they adequately administer civil and criminal law and handle the growing problems of juvenile delinquency? Can they afford the trained staffs and the facilities necessary for these purposes? Are they serving a worthwhile purpose? Numerous choices might here be considered. The

129

Johnson-O'Malley Act of 1934 could be expanded to allow the United States to contract with states to enforce law on a reservation when a tribe so requests. An act of 1953 offers means by which a state of its own motion can take responsibility for criminal and juvenile administration. Federal legislation could be sought to allow tribes to use federal staffs and facilities in the execution of juvenile codes. The tribes in an area might join in an adequate program of their own. Or they could abandon all their governing functions and agree to be regulated solely by state law.

The widespread practice of supporting Indian governments out of the income from the lease or sale of resources tends to lull the tribesmen into forgetting that their government is costing them money, something they would know if they paid taxes. Moreover, the tribes, as they increase their expenditures, lag in installing modern financial controls. With all this, however, should go increased freedom in the management of their affairs.

Though the IRA was intended eventually to give tribes greater control over their governments and business, at the time these constitutions and charters were adopted the Indians had had little experience in these respects. The Secretary of the Interior was therefore empowered to review many actions of the fledgling governments, such as law and order ordinances, taxation, appropriations, and contracts involving substantial expenditures. As a result, the secretary still maintains rigid oversight of even minor tribal actions. Indeed, even where such supervision is not required, the Indian Service reaches virtually the same result by minute scrutiny of budgets and expenditures. The tribes would progress faster if these restraints were abandoned in some cases and sharply relaxed in others. The United States, however, should not be liable for a tribe's mistakes in fulfilling its new responsibilities.

No simple procedure now exists to enforce outside the

130

reservation a civil judgment of a tribal court. Such a judgment may therefore prove actually unenforceable against an Indian who moves away. This reduces the effectiveness of the only courts to which Indians of some tribes may go for civil redress in offenses that occur on the reservation. This inadequacy could be eliminated by allowing the tribal decree to be recorded in a county office for enforcement as a state judicial decision. Though federal legislation might be sufficient to permit this, state action would make the system more acceptable to local officials and give it a greater chance to operate successfully.

Not only are tribal courts usually conducted by judges without legal training, but professional lawyers are often denied the right to practice before them. A person who is dissatisfied with the outcome, in a case involving civil liberties, should be able to appeal to a tribunal outside the tribal system, one presided over by a trained judicial officer. Why retain a system that doesn't function properly?

Except where Congress has expressly limited a tribe's jurisdiction, as with the ones in Oklahoma, state laws do not extend to a reservation Indian or his holdings or to the collective tribal property. Major offenses on a reservation, however — murder, manslaughter, burglary, larceny, arson, rape, incest, embezzlement of tribal funds, and serious assaults — rate as federal crimes if involving an Indian or Indian property. Lesser offenses of the members fall under tribal law and are tried in the tribal courts. Off the reservation an Indian is subject to the same law as are all other persons.

In a deviation from the rule, Public Law 280 in 1953, as amended, allowed state laws to supersede tribal and federal enactments concerning reservation Indians in Wisconsin, Minnesota (except Red Lake Reservation), Nebraska, California, and Oregon (except Warm Springs Reservation). The states may not, however, tax or regulate or determine the use or ownership of restricted Indian property. The statute further permitted any other state to

131

extend its criminal and civil legislation to Indians on its own say-so.

President Eisenhower, believing the measure to be a step toward complete Indian equality, approved it, although with "grave doubts as to the wisdom of certain provisions." Section 6 and 7, he said,

> . . . permit other states to impose on Indian tribes within their borders the criminal and civil jurisdiction of the state, removing the Indians from federal jurisdiction, and, in some instances, effective self-government. The failure to include in these provisions a requirement of full consultation in order to ascertain the wishes and desires of the Indians and of final federal approval, was unfortunate.

He thereupon recommended that at the earliest possible time the act be amended to require both prior consultation with the tribes and approval of the federal government. Most of the tribes for their part argued for consent as well as consultation, but the Department of the Interior opposed this. Neither the president's urging nor the Indians' objections have yielded any results.

Under this law a state can now summarily take this drastic step without considering the consequences to the Indians (which the states have), without providing any safeguards against the discrimination which exists in some places, and without setting any standard for the services to be performed. Indeed, in the case of the Omaha Indians in Nebraska, neither the state nor its subdivisions furnished adequate policing after the United States withdrew.

Few states have in fact taken any action under this measure. South Dakota did so only on the impossible condition that the United States defray the costs, something the statute does not permit; hence, the state has not assumed the responsibility.

The experience of the state of Washington points the

moral. Its legislature considered a bill to impose its jurisdiction without Indian consent. The Indians almost unanimously objected and the measure was defeated. Then at the 1957 session they successfully backed a bill which met their desires. It allows the state to assume the responsibility only after a tribe, through its regular processes, has petitioned the governor to extend state law to its reservation. Eleven tribes on their own initiative have so acted. (Later the entire Indian country went over.)

If the government feels that the Indians need a separate local government, it should defray the expenses. Otherwise, the Indians are paying for one extra government that really doesn't add to their welfare.

In the long run, it all comes down to personal suitability — whether one councilman is elected or not really doesn't matter. There are good councilmen and poor ones. One Indian described his councilman as "nice old fellow, he don't do much, he sit like stove with all the dampers closed." There is corruption in some councils, too — inevitably — though only in a small way and in rare cases. Perhaps the councilman can make sure his relatives get houses out of the welfare fund. But election time comes around every two years. In Canada, however, the parliamentary committee chaired by Indian Senator James Gladstone has recommended that the period of office be increased to three years and only half the council be elected each time, so as to ensure some continuity. One of the problems is that few Indians have any experience of administration, and a council meeting can be a pretty dreary affair if the chairman doesn't keep it under control. In the United States, most reservations have two-year terms which are staggered, ensuring a form of continuity. The women of some tribes weren't allowed to vote until recently. There is a new trend developing now; women are allowed to vote. In Canada you can find women chiefs. This sort of thing certainly goes over big with the women. Of course, if a

133

woman has the ability and intelligence, she'll get people to vote for her.

In theory, everything concerning the running of the reservation is determined by the business council. Disputes are settled, grievances heard, bylaws are made. If the tribal funds allow, various welfare and road building funds are set up and administered. If there is a housing fund, the council must decide which families deserve housing loans.

In Canada, if there is no housing fund, the band depends on free government housing from the Indian Affairs Branch. The council recommends the deserving welfare cases. Two funds for each band are held by Ottawa: a capital fund, composed mainly of money from capitalized annuities and the sale of reservation land; and a revenue fund which the band mainly builds up itself. It can accrue from interest on the capital fund, income from reserve land leased to non-Indians, income from oil wells or share-cropping deals, and from sales of timber. The Hobbema Reservation in Alberta has fifty-six producing oil wells, and its revenue fund is so healthy that the council recommended giving every man, woman and child on the reservation, fifty dollars a month. However, other reservations have no valuable land, no timber, no oil; so their revenue fund is small.

However, in Canada, this income doesn't go straight into the Indians' pockets. It goes into the revenue fund, which is released by the federal government to the band only for specific purposes approved by the Indian Affairs Branch. The budget each year is spent on such things as telephone and electricity installations on the reservation, loans to help band members build houses, welfare payments during times of unemployment, and so on. However, the Indian Act does provide for limited administration of the revenue fund by the band itself, if the band requests this privilege. In this case, the band council draws a budget for the coming year. Money for those items approved by the

134

government is deposited in the local bank account. And then the council issues its own checks for the already approved expenditure.

Even when the tribe administers its own funds, it is token control at best. The Indian's program of expenditures must be approved, and then, if he wants to, he can sign his own checks. And yet, very few tribes have elected to handle their own funds even to this limited extent. The major stumbling block is education. Most Indians haven't the education or the experience, so they lack the confidence to even try to handle their own affairs in this very limited way.

Everything concerning the running of the tribe and the reservation is determined by the business council — in theory. But in fact, all the decisions, all the plans and resolutions are subject to federal government scrutiny and final approval. In many cases it doesn't have to go as far as Ottawa or Washington, because nearly every reservation has a government representative on the spot — or if not on the reservation, then in the nearest town. He is known as the superintendent. Many Indians complain that in practice he is really the chief. This brings us to the role of the federal government in the Indians' life.

The branch or bureau responsible for Indian affairs is divided into a number of divisions such as agencies, responsible for field operations and trusts, which look after Indian lands and funds; education which caters to young and old; economic development responsible for job placement, training and wildlife; and welfare, which is self-explanatory. The Bureau of Indian Affairs in the United States is not responsible for health and medical services to Indians. This is the concern of another department.

Just as to most white folks, a government agency is something pretty mysterious and very remote. The important part of the government to my people is the Indian superintendents. They are so important that the whole

135

course of my people's lives depend on them. I don't think they know it. They can either work with you, help you learn, show you the right way to get what you want; or they can act like the big boss and tell you what you can't do, thereby taking all the initiative and self-respect away from you.

In olden days most agents never had respect for Indians. Some of my people would go to his door. Most of the time the agent would slam the door in the Indian's face.

My objection to the Indian Service provided by the government is the manner in which they pick their personnel. These people have no knowledge of the Indians' problems. Furthermore, they have no way of knowing how to deal with the Indian population.

In Canada, the local government official is called the Indian superintendent. He is the counterpart of the native administrator in many other parts of the world, but with this essential difference, that elsewhere administrators are responsible for groups that are preponderantly native; whereas in Canada, the Indians comprise only approximately one percent of the total population. The Indian superintendent is concerned with raising the economic, social, and educational standards of this small ethnic group to the general level of the Canadian population. And within his own particular unit or agency, the superintendent is responsible for upwards of three thousand Indians, to whom he must be guide, counsellor, and legal interpreter; but he must be much more than that. In any given day the superintendent may be called upon to advise on a wide variety of subjects — agriculture, mining, forestry, fishing, and many other pursuits from which the Indians derive a living.

At the same time, he will be called upon to organize band councils and committees, supervise elections, plan housing developments, and provide social welfare assistance wherever necessary. He is responsible for seeing that every child in his care receives a full and proper education and placement in employment. A superintendent's life is one

136

of constant pressure — pressure from the Indian people who feel he should be doing more for them; from the general public who feel he should be doing his job differently, and often pressure from government treasury officials who feel that he should be doing his work more economically.

Most of the superintendents now are fine men. They are dedicated to helping the Indian in every way. However, some are men with no manners, who'll send for you and keep you waiting all day, men who haven't got time to see the Indian, who wants advice on a problem, men who shout at you as if you were children, or talk about you as if you weren't there.

There are complaints that some Indian superintendents could do a lot more to explain government policy to the people in their areas, to straighten out misconceptions, and to smooth out resentments. These men are civil servants and owe their loyalty to superiors, but many Indians feel they could be more active in helping to fight infringements of Indian rights. Many Indians, too, sometimes even feel their privacy is being invaded when the superintendent attends their meetings — sometimes even takes the chair. It is often suggested that Indians themselves would make better superintendents on the reservations.

Perhaps a good starting point would be to appoint the council chairman or chief to the office of superintendent. Generally there are men more capable on the reservations to handle these affairs; individuals whose experience gives them complete knowledge of local affairs. The Indian could do it, provided he had the proper education and experience.

The frequent argument used is that if an Indian were superintendent, some of the Indians would be prejudiced about him being over them. A bunch of Indians can run down a white superintendent, and it is no skin off anybody's nose. But when a bunch of Indians run down another Indian, they may not stop at running him down. They don't want to see another Indian just a shade better

137

off than they. It is easy enough to criticize, and a great many Indians and a great many non-Indians indulge in this luxury. At times there are valid criticisms, however.

Government Policies Toward Indians

Does the white voice of authority suppress the Indian, taking away his rights and his self-respect? Or does it simply protect, taking away initiative and self-confidence? Or is it justifiable — a necessary guidance to a people who need help?

Now let us turn to the federal government organizations and its interdepartment relations in the United States.

Organizational arrangements of the Department of the Interior and its relationship to other departments in the federal government; to Indians, to the tribal governments, and to the internal structure of the Indian Service are what we are concerned with now.

Over the years Indian affairs have been spread among federal departments to a greater extent than is commonly

139

realized. The Extension Services, with a few exceptions, are now supervised by the Department of Agriculture. The responsibility for Indian health was transferred from the Department of the Interior to the Department of Health, Education and Welfare. In 1962 about one-fourth of the total federal expenditure on behalf of my people was disbursed by the Indian Health Division of the Public Health Service. Additional sums appropriated to the Department of Health, Education and Welfare were used for the benefit of Indians and others under programs of federal aid to education such as Public Laws 815 and 874.

This distribution of functions raises serious questions of uniformity in such administrative areas as budgeting, program planning, coordination of eligibility standards, and relationships with state governments.

An interdepartmental liaison committee should be formed with representatives from the departments of the Interior; Health, Education, and Welfare; Agriculture; the Bureau of the Budget, and the Attorney General. This committee would meet regularly to ensure uniform standards and program coordination.

No one organization speaks for all Indians. No one organization represents all the varied interest groups which are attempting to help the government and my people find solutions to their problems. My people and their friends frequently find themselves pitted against other special interest groups concerned with mineral exploration and development, power, timber, grazing, and water. There has never been complete agreement as to the objectives and programs among those concerned with Indian affairs, and the lack of it has made it difficult for the department to fulfill its mission.

From 1869 until 1933 the Secretary of the Interior was assisted in the performance of his duties by a Board of Indian Commissioners, set up by statute, appointed by the president, and provided with modest appropriations. A board of advisors or commissioners should again be created, with the objective of aiding the secretary, improving administration, and broadening representation.

If handled properly such a board could conceivably replace the Bureau of Indian Affairs. The previous board was created in 1869 because of scandalous practices by Indian agents in the purchase of supplies. The modern Indian Service, with its system of inspection and audits and its programs of technical assistance, bears little resemblance to the bureau of a century ago.

On the other hand, other government agencies, including some in the Department of the Interior — such as the National Park Service — have found it helpful to be guided in their activities by an advisory board with statutory authority and an appropriation. In 1950 the Indian Service had such an advisory board, based upon secretarial rather than statute authority.

The Department of the Interior needs to improve public understanding of Indian affairs, and this can be partially accomplished through more citizen participation in Indian affairs at all levels. In addition, the Indian Service can benefit from the advice of interested and public-spirited citizens, both Indian and non-Indian. Furthermore, continuous policy research is needed in the normal evolution of the Indian Service and the Department of the Interior. This type of activity would assure that the Indian is getting his fair share of government expenditures.

Operating under delegations of authority from the Secretary of the Interior, the Indian Service is one of the oldest units in the federal government. It antedates the department itself, and is steeped in custom and tradition. It is an honorable service, but it also has its share of scalps and skeletons. It has been studied repeatedly, most recently by the Bimson group in 1953, and a few years previously by the management firm Booz, Allen and Hamilton.

Since the Bimson report, the Indian Service has been organized on a three-level, three-line basis. The central

141

office in Washington, with about four hundred employees, is responsible for overall direction, planning and programming, coordination, inspection and evaluation. The intermediate level, consisting of ten area offices, has broad delegations of authority, as well as supervisory responsibility over the field installations. Direct services to Indians are provided through five hundred large and small field installations, which are headed by some forty-two superintendents. Typical installations include reservations, schools, area field houses, subagencies, and relocation offices. The bulk of the Bureau's Indian Services' (more than fifteen thousand) employees are in the field, with almost half of them engaged in providing educational services.

This three-layered structure is vertically segmented by an equal number of program divisions based on the functions of administration, community services, and resource management. An assistant commissioner heads each of the latter. In general, similar divisions are found in the area offices and the field installations.

There is general dissatisfaction in the Indian country with the slow rate at which the Indian Service performs its abundant paperwork. Items initiated in the field often must move through a network of reviews and appeals all the way to the secretary's office, with numerous side trips to specialists and solicitors. Two characteristics of the Indian Service's structure inevitably produce administrative delay and poor communications between the field and central office.

The first of these is the different organizational basis for the field and central offices. In the field installations and area offices, the Indian Service is primarily organized on a geographic basis, whereas the central office is organized solely on a functional basis.

The other factor which causes delay and a breakdown in communications is the substantial internal layering of the department, which complicates the route by which

142

matters reach the commissioner and the secretary for decision. The deputy and assistant commissioners, the assistant secretary and members of his staff, as well as various persons in the solicitor's office and the secretariat, must often become involved before the commissioner and the secretary make a final decision. In similar situations, large businesses have generally found it necessary to create an operating committee composed of those whose duties are closely associated with the principal executive officer. The members of such a committee (including the legal staff) hold daily meetings, with all present in the same room at the same time, and can greatly speed up the flow of paperwork and improve communications which are vital to decision making.

Activities which should be conducted:

1. Research and analysis: A first step toward economic development is the preparation of reservation inventories. All reservations should have such inventories as a basis for sound planning.

2. Community planning and development: Successful economic and industrial development requires a favorable community atmosphere, as well as orderly provision of facilities. For example, haphazard location of buildings is not conducive to industrial or community development.

3. Recreation development: Planning and feasibility studies making use of the National Park Service's experience could contribute materially to the promotion of tourism, and tribal recreation enterprises, which take advantage of the scenery, hunting and fishing, and wilderness areas of Indian reservations.

143

4. Industrial contact: Contact with industry, trade associations, professional organizations, chambers of commerce, and state development authorities is essential to the attraction of industry to the reservations.

5. On-the-job training: Public Law 84-959 was designed to assist in developing jobs for Indians. Vocational placement in nearby communities can be helpful in the development of reservation economies.

The most frequently heard complaint about the administration of Indian affairs is related to the area offices. Critics of the area offices seek their abolition, on the ground that they interpose a barrier between my people and the department in Washington, and take away power and authority from the superintendent. Thus, these critics wish to return to the old relationship between the individual Indian and the superintendent on the one hand, and between the superintendent and the central office on the other.

They express a sense of frustration and disappointment based on the failure of many Indian Service programs to yield effective results. The red tape and the slow process affects results. The reservations and the Indian leaders are the focal point. This position should be strengthened. The needs of the reservations are changing, and the local Indian leaders, in most cases, are ready for swift economic and cultural advances.

The area offices are intermediate command institutions, which serve a duplicate function. Every government agency with a central office, regional offices and field installations has similar problems. Indian affairs behoove us to cut back the administrative costs, and put the money into rehabilitation of reservation lands and training of the Indian people.

144

There should be maximum delegations of authority to the reservation, with a clear understanding that, to the fullest extent possible, these delegations are to be passed on to the local Indian leaders. The role of the superintendent's office in providing technical services which cannot be practically provided by the tribal organizations ought to be clearly defined. Appeals should not be permitted to delay or to avoid difficult decisions.

The location and jurisdiction of the area offices are not always in accordance with principles of good management. The Indian Service should be reservation oriented, with clearly defined checks and balances to establish responsibility in a graphic and real sense. Then the Indian can be shown his place and his responsibility, now and when he ultimately is on his own.

The selection of superintendents is one of the major functions of the upper levels of the Indian Service and the Department of the Interior. The superintendent is a field agent who should have maximum on-the-spot decision-making authority. Wherever there was an understanding superintendent working in harmony with effective tribal leaders, economic development was in operation, increased job opportunities, improved housing, and lifted Indian morale.

On the other hand, in an organization as large as the Indian Service, dealing with complex problems of human relations, there are bound to be some superintendents whose attitudes and actions arouse dislike, lack of confidence, and resistance among the Indians. A formal procedure could be found to identify in advance superintendents who can work well with Indians and those who cannot. However, the difference in results is plainly visible on the reservations. Perhaps a prediction can best be made on the basis of previous success in working with my people in other field positions, but not in forestry. The day of the wooden Indian must pass if success is to come.

A superintendent should demonstrate that he can handle

145

authority before a full delegation is given to him. Only those who have demonstrated their ability to receive and carry out full authority, and to work successfully with my people, ought to continue as superintendents.

No man should be placed as a superintendent without a period of in-service training. The practice, which seems to have been followed in many cases, of promoting men to superintendent positions from technical or professional employees who have made good records in their special fields, is of doubtful validity.

Furthermore, when good superintendents are found, there should be a way to reward them in place, rather than move them to other jobs which are rated more highly because they spend more money or have more employees. A superintendent at a small agency may actually have a more difficult task, and perhaps more acute problems, than the superintendent at a larger reservation with a correspondingly larger staff. The Indian Service and the Department of the Interior should explore the possibilities of promoting superintendents in place. Furthermore, as in the Foreign Service, Indian Service employees might be given ratings which they could carry with them from one assignment to another, thus providing more administrative flexibility.

Many differences exist in salary schedules and housing accommodations from reservation to reservation, and among employees of the Indian Health Division and the Indian Service and the Indians on the same reservations. Such differences adversely affect employee and Indian morale. The Indian Service cannot be expected to become a real "Indian service" unless proper accommodations are provided for the Indians on the spot. Also, salary schedules should be made more equitable for Indian Service employees, and contracts with other administrators in the same field or related fields should be systematically encouraged. The superintendents should have annual conferences for education and coordination purposes.

Full Indian participation in American life requires the

146

collaboration of my people, the American people, and government officials at all levels. Since at present many persons outside the Indian Service view Indians and their problems in terms of stereotypes based on myths, anachronisms, and deliberate distortions there is serious need for a major public relations effort which will acquaint the American people with the Indian as he is today. There is a need also to relate the history and present status of his problems, and the programs which the federal government and other agencies have instituted in his behalf.

Indian Service employees everywhere should consider public relations one of the most important of their responsibilities. Superintendents should not only accept invitations to discuss their work, but should undertake to create opportunities for such discussion. Regular appearances before service clubs, chambers of commerce, and women's organizations should be a required part of the responsibility of all superintendents, members of their staffs, and the local Indian leaders.

Considerable variation exists from reservation to reservation in the kinds of information materials which are available for distribution to the public. In a few places, office staffs had prepared small booklets summarizing pertinent data for each reservation and including small maps showing reservation locations. These are extremely useful, but the statistical information which they contain does not always agree with that included in publications prepared by the central office. Apparently, this calls for more coordination, and constant updating of statistical materials.

In view of the great American interest in my people and the vast quantity of misinformation circulated by other sources, the Indian Service should have available at all times a large reservoir of books, pamphlets, photographs, color slides, motion pictures, recordings and, conceivably, videotapes, which could be utilized by Indian Service personnel at all levels; by teachers, newspapers, radio and

147

television stations, lecturers and others. Members of Congress could certainly find a use for such materials, both to circulate among their constituents and to employ for committee briefings. The availability of this information in a condensed, palatable form would be of great value in the Indian Service's program for training new employees.

If we are to enlist the aid of local agencies of government, the non-Indians near the reservations, and the American public generally in helping solve Indian problems, it is absolutely crucial that all necessary steps be taken to inform these individuals and agencies concerning the nature of these problems.

If an adequate amount cannot be appropriated for a sound Indian Service information program, then the Department of the Interior should consider approaching some of the foundations which have given aid to the U.S. Information Agency, the National Park Service and other bureaus faced with similar problems. In fact, the U.S.I.A. and the Indian Service might work together in preparing some information materials, since there is almost as much interest in Indians outside the country as within. The need for a strong information office in the Indian Service can't be overstated.

Tribal organizations should be encouraged to develop information programs of their own. A few have done this with notable success. For example, one of the most useful films now available was produced by the Indians of the Fort Apache Reservation. If tribal organizations can develop their own materials and make them available to the Indian Service, the interests of both the Indians and the federal government will be better served.

Legal matters for the Indian Service are handled through the office of the solicitor of the Department of the Interior. Although representatives of this unit are located in the field, many items must be referred to the central office for decision. This procedure is aptly described as a "major bottleneck." This is especially true with respect to the approval of attorney's contracts.

Since the Indian Service's operations are far-reaching and often involve legal questions, the help of the solicitor must frequently be sought. However, too many of the matters sent to the solicitor require administrative, rather than legal, decisions. Furthermore, the secretary should not, under any circumstances, permit the Indian Service to avoid its responsibility by shifting decision-making to the legal staff.

Opinions on some subjects are so divided that they are unable to reach a satisfactory conclusion. In general, members of the solicitor's staff supported the present system, whereas the Indians and some of the Indian Service personnel indicated preference for the former system. My people especially insisted that under the present arrangement their viewpoints are not given adequate attention, especially when the Indian Service has a legal dispute with some other branch of the Department of the Interior.

Any consideration of federal-state relationships in the field of Indian affairs must begin with the basic legal doctrine that the Congress of the United States, under the Constitution, has plenary power over Indian tribes. The "commerce clause" of the Constitution, empowering Congress to regulate commerce with the Indian tribes, provides a foundation for the vast structure of treaties, federal laws, and judicial decisions affecting Indians. The corollary of this doctrine of plenary power is that the Congress has authority to repeal, abrogate or amend any of the treaties, even though these are called the supreme law of the land. It has been hard for some of the tribes to accept this conclusion. The taking of Indian land, as in the case of the Kinzua Dam, may be in direct violation of a promise in the treaty that the United States would not take Indian land until my people were ready and willing to surrender it. However, there is no question of the power of the Congress to take the land.

149

Most of the state enabling acts and state constitutions, in recognition of the federal authority, contain a disclaimer over Indians and Indian lands, to the following effect: "Said Indian lands shall remain under the absolute jurisdiction and control of the Congress of the United States." Even the constitution of Alaska, the newest of the states, has such a provision.

In short, except as the Congress has transferred its authority to the states, the states have no jurisdiction over Indian reservations or Indians on the reservations. My people away from the reservations, on the contrary, are subject to the state laws.

Congress has transferred some of its powers either by general statutes or by statutes applying to particular areas or tribes. Descent and distribution of Indian property traditionally have been governed by the laws or customs of the tribes. Congress, however, in the General Allotment Act of 1887, provided that allotments made thereunder should be probated "according to the laws of the state or territory where such land is located." The states' power to act, nevertheless, is almost nil, for in the Probate Act of 1910 Congress gave the Secretary of the Interior the power to approve wills, determine heirs and partition allotments.

Other fields in which Congress has acted are health and education. State quarantine and sanitation regulations are applicable to Indian reservations under regulations prescribed by the Secretary of the Interior. State compulsory school attendance laws may also apply to my people on reservations, but only if the council or other governing body of the tribe has adopted a resolution or ordinance giving consent to such application (which is ridiculous).

Another general statute is on major crimes which the Supreme Court has also held applicable to the Indian country. The effect of that statute is to make criminal actions, as defined by state laws, subject to federal prose-

150

cution if they are committed on lands under the exclusive jurisdiction of the United States, even though the acts are not crimes under federal law.

Finally, the Act of August 15, 1953, popularly known as Public Law 280 (83rd Congress), gave the consent of Congress to the assumption of jurisdiction over Indians to five named States: California, Minnesota, Nebraska, Oregon, and Wisconsin (with one reservation each excepted in Wisconsin and Minnesota). The act further gave the consent of Congress to any other state which, by legislation or constitutional amendment, wished to assume jurisdiction over my people.

Over the passing years, especially since 1924, federal-state relations affecting my people have greatly changed. Historically, there is support for the contention of some of the states that my people were exclusively a federal responsibility. So long as the United States treated the tribes as sovereign, though dependent, nations, and negotiated and ratified treaties with them, there was little or no occasion to negotiate with the states about Indian matters. As a result of various special acts, many Indians had become citizens by the early 1920s. In the First World War, reservation Indians generally were not subject to the draft, but hundreds of them volunteered and gave valiant service. Partly in acknowledgment of this record, Congress in 1924 declared all native-born Indians to be citizens of the United States. Forthwith, all Indians also became citizens of the states in which they reside, entitled to all the services and protections as are other citizens.

Not all the states immediately accepted this changed situation. Even in the basic matter of voting rights, some of the states, on one pretext or another, denied my people the right to vote. Not until 1948 did the last states, Arizona and New Mexico, give in as the result of decisions of the courts. Utah, for a brief period in 1956, refused to establish polling places on the reservation, but after the Indians

151

carried their case to the Supreme Court, the legislature promptly repealed the old statute on which the state attorney general had relied.

Education, welfare and relief assistance under social security, law and order, hunting and fishing, and trespass are some of the fields in which the Indian Service may deal with the states and their subdivisions. At the same time the points of contact with the states have been multiplying, other federal agencies have taken over some of the Indian Service's functions, or have created new ones. The result has been not only that the people have lost much of their isolation, but that the Indian Service, too, has had to deal with other federal agencies, and is no longer the sole federal unit concerned with my people.

Inevitably, in such diffusion of functions there has been confusion and often injustice. With some exceptions, the general trend of state and local policy has been to resist or refuse to act, unless the federal government, through the bureau or otherwise, makes a monetary contribution. Thus, under authority of the Johnson-O'Malley Act of 1934, the Indian Service has been making payments to the states for the education of Indians in public schools. The theory under which such payments are made has shifted with the years, but basically the payments make possible services which the community or the state says it cannot afford to provide. One of the stock arguments is that Indians pay no taxes on their trust or restricted lands. This argument may have some validity in the states whose principal financial base is the tax on real property, but it is heard with equal vigor in states whose governmental functions are supported by state income taxes, sales taxes, excise taxes, licenses and fees, all of which are paid by my people. The passage of Public Laws 815 and 874, with the subsequent amendment qualifying Indian trust or restricted lands as "federally impacted areas," has made possible the construction and operation of many public schools which would otherwise not have been available to Indians.

152

The status of my people away from the reservations is frequently a cause of argument between the states and local governments on the one side, and the Indian Service on the other. My people may be living away from the reservations, yet not have qualified under state laws or county and municipal ordinances, for assistance of various kinds given to other citizens. Such Indians may not have lost their rights as tribal members. They would be entitled to Indian Service assistance if they returned to the reservation, but return may not be desirable. The whole problem of eligibility, whether for medical care, education, general assistance of relief, or any other service, is a vexing one.

If my people meet the requirements established for citizens generally, they are legally entitled to receive the benefits and rights of citizenship. However, a medical plan of partial payment should be instituted throughout the Indian country. This plan can be expanded for all citizens if it is operative.

Water rights under the laws of seventeen western states derive from the doctrine of "beneficial use." In general, the principles which underlie this doctrine are that all the water in the state belongs to the people; that it may be assigned by the state from one user to another; and that the right to water is not a vested right appurtenant to the land, but an appropriative right subject to administrative regulation.

A clear statement of this basic proposition is illustrated by Article 16 of the constitution of New Mexico, which provides that "beneficial use shall be the basis, the measure, and the limit of the right to the use of water." Either the constitutions or the statutes of Arizona, Colorado, Idaho, Nevada, New Mexico, Oregon, South Dakota, Utah, Washington, Wyoming, and perhaps some other states as well, provide that the water in all rivers, streams and other sources belongs to or is owned by the public or the state.

Other states in which water rights are of importance

153

recognize the "riparian" doctrine, which holds that the owner of land on the banks of a stream is entitled to the beneficial use of the water as it flows past. Riparian rights are repudiated in toto in Colorado, Arizona, Idaho, Montana, Nevada, New Mexico, Utah and Wyoming. The riparian doctrine is recognized in varying degrees in seven western states, repudiated in the above eight, and is unclear in two.

Nonuse of water to which a right is asserted results in abandonment of the right under the state laws of Arizona, Idaho, Nevada, Oregon, Utah, New Mexico, and North and South Dakota.

In the seventeen western states where beneficial use is the basis of water law, my people are a minority which has been overwhelmed by stronger, more technologically advanced and more politically influential populations which have taken and used waters desired and claimed by the Indians. Since this has been permitted by states, and most of the available water has been thus appropriated by non-Indians, it is too late for Indians to obtain water under state law.

In the light of the above, it is not surprising that Indians rely on doctrines of federal laws and litigation in the federal courts for the assertion of their rights. By extensive litigation which has been carried repeatedly to the Supreme Court, it has been established that, in creating Indian reservations, the United States intended for the Indians an amount of water sufficient to supply all the irrigable land within the reservation boundary, as well as to provide for associated domestic, stock, and related water uses. Reservation of this amount of water is implied and need not be expressly stated by treaty, statute, or executive order. It is a vested property right appurtenant to the Indian land. The priority of the right is the date the reservation was established. The existence of and the continuation of such right is not dependent upon actual use of the water

154

at any given time; and it continues even though others may have taken and used the water after the reservation was created.

This view of Indian water rights, which has repeatedly been asserted by the federal courts, is in conflict with the doctrine of water law in the western states and with the prevailing mood in water-short areas, particularly in times of severe drought. It is also clear that most of the Indian water rights are based on federal court interpretations which do not have much statutory implementation.

One example of the strategic importance of prevailing Indian water rights is the Navajo Irrigation Project. This project would have been impossible if Section 9 of the Navajo-Hopi Rehabilitation Bill had been adopted in 1950. The intent of this section was to extend state, civil, and criminal jurisdiction to the Navajo Reservation. In spite of urgent Navajo needs and the importance of the total Navajo program, President Truman vetoed the bill. His principal reason was the fact that the attorney general was unable to assure him that in the event of litigation over water rights, he would be successful in removing the case to the federal courts where the doctrine of paramount Indian water rights would prevail. The Congress wisely removed the objectionable section and repassed the Navajo-Hopi bill, thus paving the way for the Navajo Irrigation Project and, incidentally, for other greatly enlarged Navajo programs which were unforeseen at that time.

It has been asserted from time to time that my people's fears about the loss of water rights under state jurisdiction are groundless in view of the language in Public Law 83-280. This statute, which grants to the states the option of extending civil and criminal jurisdiction to Indian reservations, provides that nothing in the act shall "alienate" existing Indian water rights. The amount of protection which this statute provides is uncertain, since it does not specify what the existing Indian water rights are. My people

155

fear that if disputes over these rights were litigated in state courts, the doctrine of beneficial use would decide the issue. In such cases their only recourse would be prolonged in costly litigation in the federal courts.

It is not suggested that Indian land should remain undeveloped. On the contrary, Indians should use their water rights to the fullest extent. To do so would provide a source of income and, at the same time, would be a practical protection of their rights.

Therefore, it would be improvident to remove federal jurisdiction over Indian water rights until the irrigable acreage of a given reservation has been determined; until the quantity of water needed and its priority have been definitely fixed; and until federal laws giving ironclad protection against losses have been enacted.

Because Indian water rights are definite in the decisions of the federal courts but uncertain in their work-a-day application, the Indian Service bears a heavy responsibility to be at all times a vigorous defender and developer of what is perhaps the most valuable of all of my people's assets.

Needed Indian Legislation and Proper Implementation

The Indian country is most often associated with Indian reservations. Because most of my people live on reservations, the reservation is their life. It is where they were born, where they spent their childhood, and where many of them live even if they do go to work in the city. The reservation is still the place most of them think of as home.

There are reservations with poverty and dirt, reservations with thirty thousand dollar houses. There are some with a farming economy, or ranching. There are some just like suburban housing developments. And there are primi-

157

tive reservations with disease and discomfort in tar paper shacks.

The woods are still there, and the ducks, and the fish. But where the Indians used to live in tents or log cabins, or shacks, now there are houses. Some are in a bad state of repair, some are new houses built by the team of carpenters employed by the tribe. The houses are spread out for the most part, served by dirt roads rather in the fashion of other country communities. Most of the shopping is done in the neighboring town. Regardless of their financial situation, they nearly all have cars of some type. Transportation is an essential in rural areas, not a luxury. Most reservations are within reach of towns and cities.

There are other kinds of reservations. The more remote country reservations are away from industry, maybe within reach of a small town, with a farming or ranching economy. The layout is roughly the same. Some land is cleared for farming. Houses are well separated. Maybe there is one small grocery store; maybe not. Some of my people have small holdings, some live on relief, and a few are really successful farmers.

In Canada not all reservations are occupied — eighteen hundred of them are in British Columbia, where some tribes have different reservations set aside for fishing, hunting or berry picking in season. Some reservations, like Desoronto or Sarnia, are near metropolitan areas. Their residents earn good incomes and the houses may be hardly distinguishable from other suburban districts. But farther north, where the weather is harder and the terrain less hospitable, the standard of living is lower. Where power dams or construction projects or mining towns are near enough to the reservation, the Indians mix with the worst sort of non-Indian, and there is often considerable moral deterioration.

Generally their housing is very poor. They are exceptionally poor as a matter of fact. They consist of slab-wood shacks mostly, old cyanide drums cut up to make the roof.

158

Actually they are not third-grade but about fifth-grade housing. When you see all this, it makes you realize, or it should make the average person that is thinking at all realize, that economically these people are in a bad way. Somehow they get money for liquor and beer; when they should be spending it on the proper nutrition and foods for their children, and better clothing, or trying to improve their housing.

In many trapping and fishing areas, the houses may mostly be made of logs, with a few made of new frame construction. There the people wear the parkas and fur jackets and clothing made of skins to suit the climate. And farther north still, there are people who live in tents, moving from place to place and following the animals which supply their food and clothing. So you see, there are many different kinds of reservations. And of course, the way of life varies, as well as the standard of living.

What are the homes like for instance? Well, sometimes you'll find an Indian who has had a good education and gets a good job. Maybe he doesn't live on the reservation, but he has a house built for his relatives. Or maybe he lives on the reservation and commutes to the city every day. And his house will be as modern and nicely furnished as his white friends. Probably he won't have a pretty garden though. And almost certainly there'll be several dogs about.

But that is the exception, however; in Canada most houses will be cheaper ones, either built by the Indian Affairs Branch and given as part of the welfare service, or built with money borrowed from the band funds. Just like white people, Indians have to borrow to buy houses. Only they can't take out a mortgage. The Indian Act (in Canada) says an Indian's real property can't be transferred outside the band and no one is going to lend money without security. So if there is not enough money in the band fund, you have to build it yourself out of whatever lumber you can get, or just go on living in a shack until the government gives you a welfare house.

In these less expensive houses, usually you won't find a great deal of furniture: a few chairs and a kitchen table; a stove — not electric, because few reservations have electricity. In the bedroom, clothes will often be hung behind a curtain, because there are no closets. And almost certainly there is a trunk or large suitcase under the bed, with some Sunday best clothes. Pictures on the walls are not very popular, except for religious pictures in some houses, or enlarged photographs of the chiefs of the band of a generation ago. If the house belongs to an older couple, more than likely there will be snapshots of grandchildren, enlargements of family groups, or a wedding picture on a side table somewhere; and probably a young man in uniform, for the Indian boys do well in the armed forces. Indian houses are as clean and neat as non-Indian houses. There are exceptions in both cases. However, there is usually a difference. They don't go much for ornament and decoration; the scant furniture is functional. Then few reservations have running water, and few Indians bother to install pumps in their wells.

These things are not as hard to come by as some people think. An Indian can buy a car, a two- or three-thousand-dollar car, with a sizeable down payment. He will pay for the car for three or four years. However, they think in order to get indoor plumbing and running water that they have to pay cash all at once. A lot of these conveniences can be purchased in the same manner as a car. If there were a training program to educate my people on how to go about obtaining these conveniences, many of them would have proper plumbing. Electricity is another bone of contention. Many bands have funds enough to pay for installation of electricity to every house on the reservation. If funds are low, often the government will meet the cost. But, the old order doesn't change fast on the reservations.

The older generation feels, if power was let in on the reservations, they would be classified as white poeple and

160

would be required to pay taxes. On one reservation there was a rumor among the older generation (some of the younger generation fell for it, too) that the minute they put their hand on the light switch, they would be electrocuted.

Perhaps some of my people are a bit old fashioned. But in many ways that is not so bad. There is a strong community spirit among my people. There is a community hall or a meeting hall on most reservations. There is always something going on. The women do a lot of organizing.

Generally the church guild or a social group or the council help the Indian community. They have Christmas hampers for the widows and the sick and old folks. They put up hampers in the Indian homes with everything in them. They do sewing and have money-raising functions. They have bingo games and raffles. They have the ladies knit sweaters and maybe make buckskin jackets and sell tickets. Then they have a bazaar.

In some cases there is not a great deal of mixing with white folks off the reservation, except at work. With more Indian children going to white schools, there are always P.T.A. meetings. However, my people are shy people, and it takes a lot of persuading to get Indian parents to attend.

However, in some communities, there are Indians on the school board. There should be more mixing socially. There is discrimination against Indians in most reservation communities. This has to be worked out among the Indians and the white folks on the scene.

There is bad and good in every race. However, it is up to the parents and the pupils themselves to get along with people other than their own tribe or race. There are not many older folks left, but they still think their people should stay Indian, stay on the reservation and keep their old customs. This makes it difficult for the young people. They think the young could get along on the reservation. They don't understand that the young have to go out and

161

learn to make a living these days. This means working off the reservation because there is no work on the reservation, unless you have good farmland. Usually my people go away during the summer months to work in apple orchards or potato fields, or pick blueberries. Most of them are gone from early spring to about the last of October. To the majority of the Indian families, this is their only source of earning money. They buy cars, televisions, etc. They could never earn enough on the reservations to buy the things that the general population take for granted. Making a living is the big problem across the Indian country. Without good farmland or logging operations, there are very few ways of making a good living on the reservation. There are handicrafts — most Indians excel at making masks and drums and costumes for their ceremonial dances — but how much money is there in it? Enough to live on? For example, how do you make a tom-tom? Cover a frame with a deerskin. The frame is made from a trunk of cedarwood. Cut a trunk of cedarwood and carve it. Carve the designs of your clan: The Wolf Clan and the Bear Clan. When Indians get older, they get more interested in making handicrafts. Then they try to sell them to the tourists. They make all kinds of things — moccasins, pipes of peace, drums and rattles. However, without mass production, Indian crafts are a mean way to earn a living.

A service station, with the addition of a building for a craft shop, could be profitable where the traffic is sufficient to support the enterprise. There is a lot of potential there on almost all reservations, but it takes capital.

The natural resources of the reservation don't always help the individual Indian, personally. Money from the sale of timber or from leases is given in per capita cash payments to members. When an otherwise barren reservation turns out to be sitting on top of an oil field, leases for oil exploration bring in only so much income. Once oil is proved and wells start producing, the tribal fund swells so fast that the members demand their share in cash. But there are critics of this, just as everything else.

A lot of them go to work off the reservation to construction jobs, but there are not too many that have a special trade of any kind; they are just general laborers. As soon as they know there is going to be a payday on the reservation they lay off their jobs. If the boss won't let them off or give them a few days leave, they quit. The checks could be mailed to them, but they feel they have to celebrate on the reservation when per capita payments are given out.

There are some reservations close enough to industrial centers for the residents to work in the cities, or even run their own businesses, and still live on the reservation. If the city is too far, then the Indians have to move to the city. It is not easy to just move into the city. It is a big decision to make. You have to be pretty sure of making a go of it first.

However, the shelter of the reservation is not much of a place of refuge. In spite of its being home, there are disadvantages. Many Indians prefer not to notice the controls, the restrictions, as long as their lives are quiet and untroubled. Others are satisfied at not being able to control their own affairs. Perhaps you don't realize these things until you have made yourself a little stake; otherwise they don't count. But the minute you make a little stake on the reservation, you can go so high and that is it. However, there is more tranquility there. It is an easier life. All people like to be free regardless of what they pay for it. They still want their freedom, their liberty. This may be a fine thing. But still the fact is that all people, regardless of racial background or nationality, still want to make their own decisions.

Therefore, the reservation is a place of refuge for those who want a quiet life. Yet, it is a place of frustration, too, a place of restriction for those who want to get ahead.

163

There are people who say Indians should be encouraged to leave the reservation if they are to take a full part in life, accepting normal responsibilities and contributing towards their country's progress. Others, particularly the majority of Indians themselves, look upon the reservation as a sacred heritage. Most Indians look upon themselves as privileged people. They'll fight hard to keep the privileges (peculiar to them) that remain. We must remember, however, it isn't easy for my people to move into the city, to integrate with the non-Indian way of life.

However, my people must realize that these are changing times within which they find themselves. The only way that they can keep abreast in this ever-changing world is to help themselves. They, also, must accept help from the non-Indian community. They must join the non-Indian community in fostering sound government Indian policy. They must learn to follow through. They must establish clear-cut objectives.

The objectives of the federal Indian program should offer proposals aimed at complete fulfillment of my people, economically, politically and socially. The objectives are:

1. To create conditions under which my people will advance their social, economic, and political adjustment to achieve a status comparable to that of their non-Indian neighbors.

2. To encourage Indians and Indian tribes to assume an increasing measure of self-sufficiency.

Since the passage of House Concurrent Resolution 108, government policy has placed more emphasis on termination. As a result, my people, fearful that termination will take place before they are ready for it, have become deeply concerned. Their preoccupation was reflected in vigorous denunciation of the so-called "termination policy." No other topic was accorded similar attention. It is apparent

164

that Indian morale generally has been lowered and resistance to transition programs heightened as a result of the fear of premature federal withdrawal. Now, many Indians see termination written into every new bill and administrative decision; and sometimes are reluctant to accept help which they need and want, for fear that it will carry with it a termination requirement. It is wiser to assist my people to advance socially, economically, and politically to the point where special services to this group of Americans are no longer justified. Furthermore, if development, rather than termination, is emphasized, Indian cooperation — an essential ingredient of a successful program — can be expected. Resolution 108 should be rescinded and a positive government stand should be taken: that as long as the grass is green, the rivers flow, the trees grow, and the sun rises there shall be no government termination of its responsibilities to my people. Nothing short of this will suffice.

My people need employment opportunities to help make it possible for them to provide many of the necessities of life which they now lack, or which are provided for them on a welfare basis. In many of the places where Indian reservations have been established, there is limited opportunity for economic advancement. Although my people nowadays are not confined to these locations, sentiment, cultural isolation, and lack of skills have rendered them reluctant to leave or unable to care for themselves adequately in other environments.

As part of a program for providing employment, maximum development of the resources of Indian reservations is a basic essential. Not all reservations, unfortunately, have much development potential; but many of those which do have resources are lying fallow. If my people are to develop these resources themselves, capital and technical assistance are required. If they are to turn the development over to others, there must be assurance that the income thereby derived will be adequate for subsistence.

165

Resource surveys and master plans are essential to programs of reservation development. It is criminal that these rudiments of management have been left undone or done poorly for so long. There have been several abortive attempts at programs of this kind during the post-World War II era, but for a combination of reasons few of them have been completed.

A serious deterrent to more adequate use of resources in some areas has been the heirship problem. As a result of action taken during the period between 1887 and 1934, many Indian reservations were broken up into small holdings, or allotments, the titles to which were placed in the name of the United States and held in trust for individual Indians. In most cases with the deaths of the original allottees, the beneficial interest in these lands passed on to the heirs in common, rather than in severalty. This is another white-man maneuver which is costing the government millions of dollars.

Consequently, there are today hundreds of small tracts of Indian land, each of which is "owned" by literally dozens of persons. Getting all these individuals to agree as to how the land will be used, or even finding many of them, is extremely difficult. As a result, much of this land is not being put to its most beneficial use. One tribal council chairman from a Great Plains' reservation stated that there are 108,000 acres within tribal jurisdiction which are producing no income whatsoever for their owners, because of the complications arising from the problem of fractionated ownership. Living conditions on this reservation are among the worst to be found in the Indian country, and the welfare burden is immense.

Legislation has been proposed which would provide authority for the Secretary of the Interior to sell or partition these badly fractionated allotments and, in the case of the latter, issue fee patents to those having a beneficial interest. Under this proposal, loan money would also be

166

made available to Indian tribes in order to allow them to purchase those tracts of land which individual Indians might wish to sell. Such legislation would quickly result in the alienation of much Indian land. Many of those who would receive fee patents are in impoverished circumstances and would want to sell their land as soon as possible. The tribe's ability to buy would often depend upon the availability of loan money from the federal government.

The solution to the problem of idle, fractionated allotments should be sought through the following devices:

1. The granting of authority to the Secretary of the Interior to transfer the beneficial interest in highly fractionated allotments from the heirs to the tribe and to arrange with the tribe to compensate the individual owners to the extent of the fair market value of the land; making use, where necessary, of a system of deferred payments.

2. The sale of fractionated heirship lands by open competitive bidding in those cases where such lands do not fit into a tribal land consolidation program and are not desired by whatever tribal enterprise is set up to manage heirship lands. Before commencing any such sale, approval should be secured from the owners of a majority of the beneficial interests in the lands involved.

3. The application of existing but unused authority for the tribe to acquire, through deferred payment where necessary, the undivided interests in fractionated tracts while the estate of an Indian is in probate.

4. The granting of authority to the Secretary of the Interior to contract timber sales and dis-

tribute the proceeds to my people who have beneficial interests in fractionated allotments. Without waiting for the consent of a majority of the owners. This will prevent loss of revenue through the deterioration of overage timber when the owners of fractionated holdings cannot be found or will not agree on the sale of that timber.

In all the above cases, except Item 2, the land would remain in trust status and guarantees against alienation be provided.

If resource development plans are to be formulated and implemented, a source of credit must be provided. The present revolving loan fund should be expanded and used primarily for reloan by the tribes to individual members for such purposes as education, housing, and the development of individually held tracts of land for small business development. For tribal programs of greater magnitude, a new and larger credit fund is required.

Another potential source of capital, which is very popular in government circles for resource development, is the judgment money from cases now pending before the Indian Claims Commission. Every effort should be made to see that this money is not dissipated on a per capita payment basis to tribal members. This is typical white man thinking. In reality the money is desperately needed for basic living expenses. My people think that the government has let them down again. The pressure from Indians living away from the reservation is often too much for tribal councils to resist, with the result that all or a substantial portion of the judgment funds is distributed to individuals.

Employment for my people has been appreciably reduced during the past several years by the decision to employ private contractors for construction work on Indian reservations, rather than having such construction done under government supervision making use of Indian labor. The latter system, known as "force account," has in some instances been the only major source of local employment available to my people. There is substantial evidence that the welfare load has increased since the institution of the new contract policy, making it, in fact, a false economy. Furthermore, my people have thus been deprived of opportunities for on-the-job training in the building trades and allied occupations, and in the operation and maintenance of heavy construction equipment.

Return to the "force account" system should be made as rapidly as possible wherever it appears practical to do so, beginning in areas where construction is contemplated and serious unemployment problems exist.

Wherever contracts are let for construction on Indian reservations, the Indian Service should insist that these contracts contain clauses giving employment preference to local *residents*. To do so will not violate executive policy with respect to fair employment practices, since the basis for employment preference will not be racial.

Many Indians have called attention to the positive contribution which the Civilian Conservation Corps made to the lives of the Indian people during the 1930s. It provided a source of employment and training and resulted in the construction of facilities which benefited the reservation population for years after the program was discontinued.

It is reasonable to assume that similar benefits could accrue to my people under a similar program now. However, the age limits should be raised where Indians are concerned, and Indians should be permitted to participate in the program while living at home, rather than necessarily in camps. Both of these latter concessions were made under the CCC.

My people object especially to the fact that Indians

169

not living on trust or restricted property are ineligible for vocational training, and that age requirements exclude middle-aged Indians who need this kind of assistance. Also, many trainees are not placed on jobs upon completion of training.

With respect to relocation, my people regard this "service" as a primary instrument of the "termination policy" which they universally fear. My people protest that, under the present relocation program, persons leaving the reservation are not given sufficient orientation. They unanimously endorse some kind of job placement activity, with emphasis on local (near reservation) employment.

Wherever possible, increased emphasis should be put on local placement, with a much higher degree of cooperation between the Indian Service and local agencies. Funds for providing necessary services to Indians being placed in communities close to the reservation should be available, just as they are for Indians being transported to distant cities.

The Indian Service should review its orientation program for those leaving the reservation and should make certain that the problems Indians will face in off reservation communities are carefully spelled out for them.

The regulation which restricts vocational training to those residing on trust or restricted property should be changed so that all those who are eligible for other Indian Service programs will also be eligible for vocational training and placement.

The age limits should be flexibly interpreted by the Indian Service in administering the vocational training program.

In recent years several industrial plants have been located on or near Indian reservations, often with such inducements as Indian Service or tribal subsidies in the form of salaries, buildings, etc. Such programs have improved the economies of several tribes, have reduced the welfare burden, and have provided important vocational training.

In some sections of the Indian country, industrial development and off-reservation placement are key programs toward reducing unemployment. Conditions on these reservations are among the most critical to be found in the country. Industrial development must be elevated to the highest plane of importance among the Indian Service's activities.

At the present time, literally thousands of American communities have undertaken programs of industrial development. The Indian Service must compete with these communities, not only in obtaining industries for the reservations and near reservation areas, but in employing experienced industrial development advisers. The budget of the Indian Service has not been sufficient to provide for a major industrial development effort.

The Indian Service should assist the tribes in setting up programs designed to prepare Indian communities for employment in industrial establishments. Past experience has shown that the routine of industrial employment is foreign to many Indian groups. A vocational counsellor on the reservation can be of great aid to tribal officials in this matter.

The Indian Service should give consideration to the establishment of a reservation economic development advisory board. Because special technical experts will be required, it is suggested that the Secretary of the Interior work out a loan of these specialists. They would serve as temporary consultants on a term not to exceed one year's time, with replacements staggered in order to maintain the continuity of the advisory group. Similar boards should also be established wherever possible at the reservation level.

In such planning, Indian Service technical assistance should be readily available, and the federal government might also help by devices used in other economic development programs, such as accelerated depreciation on capital investment, small business loans, and provision of facilities at low rentals. Some of these latter programs would require special legislation.

Few among my people depend solely on handicraft production for their livelihood, but in hundreds of families, arts and crafts are a major source of income. The Indian Arts and Crafts Board has records indicating that more than $4,000,000 has been received by the various organized crafts groups in the past ten years; and other sums, estimated at $3 million a year, are received from sales by individual Indians. It it clear that high quality craft products can readily be sold at prices which justify the time spent in their manufacture.

Recognition by the general public of their artistic merit demonstrates to the craftsman that his workmanship is esteemed, and that the art forms of the tribe or group deserve preservation in the modern world. Furthermore, these items help to promote understanding of traditional Indian ways. As expressions of Indian thought and emotions, they tell non-Indians what kinds of people Indians are.

The promotion and development of arts and crafts on a functional basis must be an integral part of the educational program of the Indian Service. Unfortunately, during the past few years, the Indian Service has withdrawn its support from many craft projects begun earlier. Various reasons have been advanced — that they are not proper activities for the Indian Service; that they cost too much money; that they are not profitable; and that they are keeping the government in business. The benefits which my people gain from continuing their arts and crafts are more than sufficient to outweigh whatever the objections may be.

The revolving loan fund is grossly inadequate for Indian credit needs, and its stated purpose is to provide credit where outside financing is not available.

Veterans living on the reservation were not able to obtain

172

veterans' housing loans because they were unemployed and did not have satisfactory credit ratings. Other Indians said that they could not get G.I. loans because they did not have a proper title to the land on which they wished to build.

In the face of apathy by both Indians and government about housing conditions in the Indian country, only three encouraging signs appear: First, that the Indian Sanitation Act offers future promise of providing clean water and sewer systems as a public health measure. Second, that in a few locations individual Indians have, through their own efforts and with the use of readily available local materials, provided themselves with self-constructed dwellings, which are weathertight, give the appearance of being cool in summer and warm in winter, safe, clean, yet generally adequate. Third, that throughout most of the Indian country, there were substandard waterless dwellings which, nevertheless, had R.E.A. power within easy reach. It seems that the same ingenuity and resourcefulness which brought electrical power to remote areas can be applied to the urgent, truly shocking, Indian housing need.

The available government housing programs which might be turned to the solution of the problem are as follows:

1. The Federal Housing Agency program of long-term, low-interest mortgage lending and mortgage support, which has been applied to the Indian country only recently. My people earnestly hope this program will continue, but they do not feel that a loan approach is likely to meet the problem as fast as it is growing, since reservation unemployment is high, most existing dwellings ought to be completely replaced, and restrictions on alienations complicated mortgage financing.

2. Veterans' housing loans which have been so helpful elsewhere under federal and state spon-

sorship, but which are subject to the same disabilities in the Indian country as FHA.

3. The Farmers Home Administration which has authority and some funds for rural home improvement.

4. The public housing program which entitles municipalities and other governmental entities to establish public housing authorities. My people feel that Indian tribes qualify under these provisions. A public housing project was developed at Pine Ridge Reservation in South Dakota. As the Indians are brought into a wage economy, similar housing programs seem to offer the best hope for a rapid improvement in the Indian housing situation.

5. Self-help housing, a device which has proven helpful in underdeveloped areas such as Puerto Rico and some of the countries within the scope of the International Cooperation Administration. Under programs of this type, technical assistance, a small amount of money, and leadership are provided groups of individuals who are able and willing to erect their own homes out of locally available materials. This approach has not often been used on Indian reservations, but my people regard it as having great potential.

The Public Housing Administration (PHA) in January 1964 earmarked under its new mutual self-help housing program, twenty dwelling units for Swinomish Indians on their reservation in the Puget Sound region of Washington State.

The mutual self-help program is aimed primarily at providing low-cost homes for my people. Yet almost eighty

174

percent of them have incomes so low as to be unable to rent dwellings in PHA's standard, federally assisted, low-rent housing. It differs substantially from the conventional program in that the Indian tenants will construct and maintain their own homes, and thus acquire an equity which can enable them to achieve ownership within a reasonable time.

Under the new program the Indian families will construct the homes under the direction of skilled construction supervisors on land supplied by the tribe. It is expected that each family will acquire at least a twenty percent equity in a dwelling as a result of its work, and with its monthly payments and maintenance labor will be able to own the home in sixteen to eighteen years. This period could be reduced by any additional equity that the tenant could acquire through additional labor or monthly payments. My people feel that this program should be broadened to encompass the entire Indian country.

Education is the Keynote

Like other rural people, progress forces my people more and more away from the reservations, more and more to the cities and industrial centers. My people find it more difficult every year to lead their old, sheltered life. They are learning the white man's way of life and the white man's standard of living. Therefore, they have to get out to work at white man's jobs. My people encounter many problems when they leave the reservation to try and make their way in the world outside. It's an unfriendly world to most of them.

Even simple things, like how to use a telephone or catch a bus or how to apply for a job, may be stumbling blocks to my people. Although they are proud of being Indians they may feel self-conscious about not knowing how to do things in the city. This is the problem that

176

Indian centers in big cities are trying to solve, with courses to teach Indians these things. The centers help them apply for jobs, and give them application forms from different business firms.

Even language makes a barrier. Living on the reservation, my people may not use English all the time. If you're on a reservation, you don't talk about the same things as city folks. A lot of Indians find it difficult to communicate with white folks, or even understand them. They don't have the general experience to write the examinations that are given by the company to prospective employees. Some of them can drive trucks or heavy equipment. But if they can't write, they can't get an operator's license.

For any of these reasons, a great many Indians are severely limited in the kinds of employment they can get. Open discrimination against my people is, fortunately, not as common as it once was. But all too often there is a feeling that the Indian is unreliable; that he's lazy; that he's only fit for the most menial tasks. Some white men will always look down on the Indian. When an Indian makes a mistake, they think every Indian is the same. When a crime is committed, it seems that the write-up in the papers about my people always has to put the word *Indian* there. To most of my people this is sort of embarrassing. It puts a hard sort of feeling among the Indian people when they see the write-up in that way. My people like to believe that they are just as human as any other race.

Even the employer who genuinely believes he is unbiased, who would be shocked if you accused him of discrimination, will often have to think twice if you ask him, "If an Indian and a non-Indian apply for the same job, which will you take on?" There are a dozen reasons why he will pass over the Indian. Indians aren't used to working to time, they are not punctual. They don't always understand instructions. They have no initiative. They are poor mixers; they are moody. This is bad for employees'

177

morale and efficiency. They quit without notice. The other men don't like working with them. They lose time through drunkenness. These may be valid reasons in some cases. The employer feels that he has the right to take on the best man for the job. Yet this is, in effect, discrimination against my people. There is social discrimination too, in restaurants and stores, hotels, even in churches near reservation communities.

When I first came back from overseas I had my uniform on; I was just newly discharged. I went into a restaurant. It happened that this restaurant was crowded and there was a lady there occupying a table by herself. I sat there and I noticed right away that she didn't feel right about it. Well, I got my order and I wanted pepper and salt. So I asked her to pass them and she just wouldn't hardly do it. After sacrificing my life for my country, I thought I could have said something right there; but I didn't say anything. My people have gone into a restaurant, the waitress would serve other customers before they would serve them; even when they were there first. Usually a salesman will serve my people as they enter, if they are coming in for business, but sometimes they just have to kind of stand aside for a little while. To a sensitive people, this is embarrassing.

Where the Indian population is high, few have jobs and drunkenness is a serious problem. Some shopkeepers refuse to serve my people at all. This isn't discrimination, they say. It is a matter of necessity. Other customers won't come in if the place is full of dirty Indians. If my people are clean, sober, then they are welcome! But it is an unfortunate fact that in some areas very few are clean, or sober. Some of the hotel operators try to combat the drunkenness; but even that is discrimination to the Indian.

However, bartenders claim that, at least with the white man, you can talk to him and try to reason with him, and if he gives you any trouble you bounce him out of the door and that's it. With an Indian, right away he wants to take on the whole house, the glasses start to fly and, before you know it, you have a minor war on your hands. You have to adopt a very strict policy. In other words, no second chances. If he can't behave the first time he comes in, he's just automatically out. Where in the white man's case, you happen to know the individual. Well, we all have our bad days, and you will overlook the situation. If he is half reasonable, you give him another chance. Is this discrimination?

It can be a lonely life, a miserable existence, if you've been used to the protection and friendship of the reservation. While you are looking for work, you don't have much money either. This is the same with the white man, but he knows he'll get a job if there is one. But my people can't always find a place to sleep. When they are lonely, hungry, and their self respect takes another knock everywhere they go, they feel like going back home, back to the reservation. They miss their family.

Another problem, and a serious one, is the fact that many Indians, especially those who have only recently left the reservation, have no idea how to go about looking for work. Many of them can't read the want ads, even if they know such things exist. Those who can and do, often don't know how to get to the place where work is advertised. Many have never heard of the employment services, though this facility is available to them, just as to non-Indians. They are entitled to unemployment benefits as long as they have built up the necessary backlog of benefits. But if they have just come from a reservation where there is no work, they have no benefits. One rewarding step forward by the Canadian federal government has been the appointment of placement officers, men whose work it is to find employment for my people, and to find qualified Indians who can hold down a job. This service was organized in 1957, and there are now placement officers in most of the larger cities. In the fiscal year 1959-1960, 231 Indians were

179

established in permanent employment. And, in addition, 1765 Indians were found temporary or seasonal jobs.

But too many Indians go into the outside world without knowing about all the help they can get. Maybe they are too proud to call at the superintendent's office to ask. Maybe they want to get away from government control. So quite often they won't find a job, and they won't know what welfare benefits they're entitled to. They have no friends, no one to talk to. So they drift down to the skid row, where there are people no better off than they. There is no discrimination there. They can get into trouble and generally do. It is not only the men, but the women get into trouble just as easily.

They usually end up in the liquor store buying this cheap ninety-cent "goof," which they call it around there, and then they are in a real problem. When they do get liquored-up or goofed-up, they just got haywire. There is no reasoning with them, particularly with women. The language becomes foul and it just becomes an intolerable situation.

There are comparatively few Indians who establish this reputation for the rest. As a result, even those with steady jobs and pleasing personalities are faced with the problem of social acceptability. Few are willing to accept this — perhaps even to themselves — but an Indian may work alongside non-Indians, share their work and even their dangers, yet not be asked to sit down with them at lunch time. He may work in an office, yet never be invited to a non-Indian home. Small wonder, then, that some, if their appearance permits, try to conceal their Indian origin. Small wonder that they tend to flock together. Instead of integrating socially, they remain apart as if they had stayed on the reservation. The statement that "the Indian is proud," reserved, suspicious of things he doesn't understand is commonplace. These very characteristics make him more conscious of his nonacceptance; even make him suspect it where it doesn't actually exist. Perhaps this is a problem that faces all minority groups, and it is to be expected. But should it be forgotten that my people, more than any other minority, have a traditional right to a place in Canada and the United States? There are many solutions for this problem — better education, training programs, and, perhaps most important, a more enlightened approach by the non-Indians. Many of my people who are happy with their lives off the reservations have no complaints.

So the process of integration is going on slowly, more slowly than some people would wish. Some will suggest abolishing all Indian privileges, forcing a full assimilation into the general life of the community. But, as has been seen, there are obstacles to this. Is this slow progress the fault of my people? Is it the fault of the white society?

If you ask people, "Do you discriminate?", no one will say they do. They agree that they treat people differently, but then there are always good reasons for doing so and that is not discrimination then, it is treating people differently. Perhaps my people don't have much of a chance. In effect, unless one agrees that Indians are inferior, how else could one explain that after three hundred years, Indians do not have a full share in our economy, other than the fact that they have been excluded from it. Anyone else with a fair chance would by now have become a major partner with the rest of society. In this consideration of the Indian in the city, the accent has been on the problems and difficulties, the trials and the loneliness. But the successes, the successfully integrated, are increasing every year. So the case of the Indian who wants to leave the reservation is far from hopeless. It is difficult, but it is improving.

My people have been forgetting their traditional skills, but they haven't been learning much of the white man's knowledge to replace them. Education is one of the most important factors in anyone's life, and this applies more especially to my people.

Everything takes education now. Even farming takes

181

education. To learn about farming and the cattle business, you have to have an education. And most Indians claim this is mainly because of muddled policy on the part of the government. Of course, we always like to blame the government for everything, but let's look at the figures.

In Canada, in 1948, there were about twenty-three thousand Indian children attending school. Ten years later there were nearly forty thousand out of a total Indian population of one hundred eighty-five thousand. In 1948, the Indian Affairs Branch employed three hundred eighty-three teachers in Indian schools; ten years later there were more than eleven hundred in nearly five hundred Indian schools. These schools are in addition to the residential schools and the day schools on the reservation, and in addition to the normal non-Indian schools which Indian children are attending in increasing numbers. In 1948 only fourteen hundred Indian children went to non-Indian schools; ten years later five times as many attend mixed classes and make friends among the non-Indian community. But still, there were only one-fifth of the forty thousand attending school. The other four-fifths still go to Indian schools and don't mix with non-Indian children. Now, you may think there can be no excuse for such a belated increase in school attendance, when education was one of the benefits promised to Indians under the treaties. Certainly, the Indians themselves feel this.

In the Canadian Treaty of 1877, it was stated that the government would pay for education, and that as long as the sun shines and rivers flow that treaty will hold. Who broke it? If they had educated us from the start, the seventy-year-old men of today would have a good education.

There were a good many complaints about Indian schools several decades ago, and they are still not popular. Children were taken from their parents' homes, often quite young, and kept in boarding schools until they reached their middle teens. Some managed to get home for the summer holidays, others didn't. In most schools, they were forbidden

182

to speak their own language, and had to work, study, play and pray in English. At some of these schools, determined efforts were made to render the situation self-supporting by raising vegetables for the kitchens. The work in the fields was done by the Indian children themselves. My people complained that more time was spent in this way and at prayer than over their schoolbooks. The results of this kind of teaching were often unfortunate. When the children left school and went back home to their reservation, they couldn't share in the life of their own people. In many cases they had forgotten much of their own language. Many of them were repelled by the squalid living conditions of their parents. They were outcasts, unsuited either to life on the reservation or to striking out on their own. The little schooling they did manage to pick up was not, as a rule, enough to enable them to get and hold more than a laboring job.

Some parents send their children to boarding schools and forget them. The children, so went the complaint, expected everything to be done for them. They won't stand on their own feet. Some of them don't like the way the Indian schools are being run, and as soon as they are sixteen they just leave.

Bad teachers, too much gardening, and not enough learning, no family life, too much restriction, regimentation foreign to the Indian character, suppression of everything that was Indian — all these complaints and more were leveled at the residential schools. In far too many cases, they were well-founded. And yet, how many youngsters today find no fault with their schools? No doubt many of the features of residential school life, which the Indians hated, were unavoidable under the then existing circumstances. The churches were accused of simply wanting to extend their influence, using the Indians as "soul fodder," one woman called it. Yet, few Indians would have learned to read and write if the churches hadn't opened mission

183

schools. And today, there are three kinds of schools the Indian child can attend — day school on the reservation, residential school, or the local non-Indian school. Education is compulsory, as with non-Indian children. There are still groups of nomads who don't live in any fixed area. It is difficult to enforce the regulation when the children can't be found, though most of them are available for some part of the year. Some reservations have their own schools run by their own school boards, and are government supervised. Most Indian schools prefer Indian teachers when they are available.

On some reservations the tribe is neither wealthy enough nor progressive enough to educate its young people. Residential schools in Canada are still mostly run by the churches.

Naturally speaking, the first surroundings for education is the home. The parents have to be the first educators in the process of bringing up their children. There are many circumstances, there are many situations where the parents cannot or do not have the facilities to take the full responsibility for their children's education. They want them to be educated, but they do not know how. So they will take their child to a boarding school; because they want them to learn, they want them to be educated.

Boarding schools are especially useful for children from small or remote reservations where there is no day school. But it is the attitude of "wanting the children to be among the white people" which is the subject of most of the controversy.

However, our children today go to high schools and to universities. They do the same work as non-Indians. Some of our children are given scholarships. They all need an education. Education is going to transform my people into prosperous agriculturists and professional businessmen and women. We can't stop progress. Education is going to change my people. The young people are growing up. It is gradually changing for the better.

184

Certainly, they learn the good and the bad, sometimes more of the bad. Indian teachers are better teachers, because their interest is with their people.

However, the simple economics of sending a child to the public school raises problems too. Many of our families are very poor. They have to earn a living. That is a problem. There are some families that have nothing; no security, no cattle, no horses. They live by getting odd jobs.

However, the big problem with the children is that they have to learn right from the start how to get along with the white children and the teachers. That is a part of education, an essential part.

Do the white people want the Indians coming to their public schools? There are extremely few cases where Indian children have either been barred from public schools, or made unwelcome by the other children. Certainly, the school board has the right to refuse admission. In some areas, even the Indian children are alcoholics. Sometimes they are dirty and smelly. Often they are late arriving, irregular attenders, and bad for the discipline of the others. But how much longer can they be excluded, when only education can cure these faults. Many school boards are only too well aware that they wouldn't have had the new wing or that extra classroom if it hadn't been for the grant from the Indian Service, paid on behalf of the Indian children attending the school. In a few more generations, perhaps, most of us will be as well educated as the white man. But what do we do now?

What do we do in situations where a teacher has been teaching school for ten years to the same children, and they just attend grade three? Where can we place the blame? Is this what happens when the teacher can't speak the Indian language? Or is the blame with the parents?

At least part of the problem is that many of my people do not speak English at home. It has to be taught to them first before any formal teaching. They have to be taught the names of things that they are going to come in contact with. Even the names of animals which they are quite familiar with, but just don't know what they are called in English. They speak their own language and, of course, they can't change it into English overnight. The government does not want the teachers to learn the Indian language, because they feel it will hinder the Indians in learning English. However, the textbooks are standard textbooks. There are Indians who never got beyond grade three. There are Indians who go on to high school and university. And yet, in theory, there is no limit to what an Indian can do. Where does the answer come from?

An Indian has a chance today to become a lawyer, or a doctor; in fact, anything he wants to be, because he has every opportunity to get that education. At least, that is the theory of it. And even if it does not work out that way, why not? If the Indian child had had his present unlimited educational opportunities — and the encouragement to make use of them — even as recently as, say, the end of WW II, how different the situation would be today.

Or does the heavy cross of blame lay on the governments of Canada and the United States? Don't they exercise wardship over my people?

When this present generation of school children grows up, perhaps the Indian will no longer have to face problems of language, of unfamiliarity with life off the reservation, the difficulty of getting a job, and discrimination. But that is in the future. There is still a lot that can be done now to help the present adult generation of Indians cope with the changing life that faces them. They can be given technical training, adult education — even the elementary education that they may have missed.

The Indian country is divided into two roads. There is the path that many of the folks take, the path of contentment and isolation on the reservation. And there is the path that seems to be getting easier all the time. As our young people get better education and learn to compete with the white man, they take a bigger part in society. But education at school isn't everything.

There is a lot to be said for the tranquility and contentment of isolation on the reservation. There is a freedom from the everyday problems and worries of the world at large that you can't help envying sometimes. And yet, it is the contentment of stagnation, isn't it? The tranquility that comes of never reading a newspaper, never competing in the job market, never feeling the need for self-improvement. Perhaps, the old folks are right. But that is not the way of our present civilization. And as the new generation of Indians learn more at school, more about the world outside the reservation and the possibilities and challenges it offers, they are finding it is not enough to live in isolation and simply follow the ways of their grandparents. They are learning that they, too, can achieve great things, that they can do anything the non-Indian can do. They are acquiring a taste for a standard of living that few have been used to on the reservation. This realization of latent possibilities is only just beginning. The compulsory elementary eduation, for now, is all the vast majority of Indian children have been exposed to.

Even in the last twenty years, some of the white man's school boards seemed to think Indian education wasn't important enough to let all Indian children attend white schools. Education given to the Indian children in the past has done little to fit them as today's adult generation to compete in the race for jobs, for a place in the sun. Employers who would not consciously discriminate against an Indian would most certainly discriminate against an "illiterate." Now the competition for jobs is keen enough without the additional handicap of a poor command of the language.

But that still leaves the problem of a complete generation of adults, most of them are fitted only for laboring

187

jobs. Most Indian adults must be content with what is left over after the white men have taken the better jobs. They are looked down on because they haven't learned how to get around in the white man's world. There is more to education than just the three *R*s. Our children must learn to be useful citizens.

Education, whether for a white man or an Indian, is the keynote.

The educated man is able to enjoy his leisure time. People will dispute this statement. However, when you come into the world of commercial enterprise, particularly in this day of mechanical invention and automation, there is very, very little field of employment left for the man who has a strong back and a weak mind. Perhaps he has enough skill in his services that somebody wishes to employ him. Perhaps the ultimate aim of every individual is to live quietly, happily, and peacefully. However, if in attaining those objectives, he is throwing an extra burden on the rest of the population, then he is not meeting his responsibilities — he is living a very selfish life.

Through education my people will be able to compete on an equal basis with his white neighbor. When the Indian does get a better education, it is going to be easier for him to participate in the community without too much difficulty. With greater and greater educational backgrounds, a great many of the Indians aren't going to be happy with the marginal life which they can eke out on the reservation. Then, by wanting something better, they are going to have to go to the cities or to the nearby towns. They will have to accept that way of life, if they are going to get the better things which their education demands that they have. My people cannot stand still. If the Indians are going to become a part of the community, they are going to have to go ahead. Where you have two cultures, your dominant white culture and your small Indian culture, the Indian culture is going to be drawn

188

into the white community. This cannot be avoided. They are going to have difficulties at times. There are going to be heartbreaks. However, this does not mean that the Indian culture will be lost. Already the Indian culture has enhanced the greater American culture. Therefore it is reasonable to assume that the contributions which my people will make will be even greater in the future.

The Indian cannot stand still. If the Indian is going to become a part of the community, he is going to have to go ahead. Few will begrudge him this chance, even though there may be misunderstandings and problems. So now, rather belatedly, there is in theory no bar to the young Indian who wants to go on to the university, or who wants to take technical training. There is no reason why the older Indian couldn't go to night school or attend full-time courses, and qualify for those jobs which were closed to him. How often can a father afford to give up even casual labor while he goes back to school to learn a skill?

The Indian of today could be helped tremendously. Such things as agriculture shows, which include everything from home cooking, schooling, and cattle, to all classes through farming life or agricultural life, could be of great value. Actually, the background of home education is competition, and until you can build up that competition you have no base from which to start. In this matter, they would form their own competition. They would realize then that they would just have to compete if they expect to get ahead in the white man's world. Agriculture shows would be one of the most important things. When you live out in the country, every other Indian is some sort of farmer or rancher.

The Blackfeet have an expression: they say, if a person is trying to get ahead, they say he is trying to turn himself into a white man. This is certainly a derogatory comment. As a result, quite a number of young people are discouraged

189

from going ahead, purely from local pressures and public opinion. They are conscious of this feeling and conform so that they will not be criticized.

A popular belief at the reservation level was aptly stated by one Indian. He spoke about the attempts being made to improve education, to get the Indians to leave the reservations, and various other aspects of administration and development that are now taking place among the Indians. He summed it up by saying that he would rather be a first-class Indian than a second-class white man. The main reason behind this type of thinking is poor education. At one time prior to the Second World War, Indians were not expected to attend school beyond the age of about sixteen years. The educational facilities did not exist on the reservation. The Indians were not given any financial assistance, in a great many cases, to attend schools for higher education off the reservation. If the family was self-sufficient, they could perhaps send their own children, but in a great many cases a brilliant student came from a very poor home and had to stop his education at sixteen years, because the finances to go any further weren't available. Even when there was educational aid, the government agencies failed to inform my people of this and many other benefits.

The ratio of Indian students to non-Indian students is not a very good sign, because we have many students, or former students, who had just as much ability and just as much, if not more, intelligence, and could have carried on. The reason for this was real once, because they didn't have the opportunity. But in the last few years, the opportunities have become more open to Indian students.

Don't get the idea that the only form of education is the formal education of the universities or even the high schools. You should remember that education of one form or another is the only hope not only for my people, but for anybody else for that matter. I think that their hopes

190

for the future can lie only with adult education programs. Although we could run into difficulties in making this available to as many people as possible, because reservations in a lot of cases are so isolated. Therefore, any program devised to get to a lot of them would have to overcome this barrier of geographic isolation. This is part of the reason why the education has taken so long to reach many reservations. Of course, any program, any adult education program, any program of community education on the reservations would have to start with the Indians themselves.

You could not come in there with a program, no matter how good; you could not come out and tell my people that this is what is going to be good for you. This is the kind of thing that we should be getting away from. This is the attitude that the early missionaries had. For example, the missionaries said, this is the way we think you should live, this is the way you have to live, you have to abandon all your old beliefs for the new. If we tried this kind of thing, we would only be perpetuating the old paternalistic attitude towards Indians: we know what is good for you, so you take it.

The Indian parents need to understand the needs of their children better, to assure that in time their children will be able to mix more easily with others off the reservation. The more education we can give them, whether they live on the reservation or off the better it will be for the reservation because the people will be able to understand their own problems better. Perhaps in time, they will be able to cope with them better. It is very difficult for them.

But sometimes when youngsters are brought up on a reservation it is not much use teaching them nursing or metal work when they don't even know how to mix with white people, have probably never seen a typewriter or used a telephone. We must provide courses to teach them how to live like city people, so that they can learn whatever

191

they need. In short, provide them with a climate for learning.

There are many ways for the Indian to improve himself if he wants to. But when you consider the number of non-Indians who flock to evening classes and vocational schools, how can we motivate the Indian? Can the government do more to encourage them? Why aren't more of them taking advantage of the help that is available? Some of the reasons might be that they didn't have the proper encouragement from their parents. They didn't get the proper encouragement in some of the schools that they attended. A lot of this stems from the fact that education, to some of my people was not necessarily a good thing.

Education is the heart of the matter; however, formal education and adult education are the golden keys to emancipation and equality. This may be true, but not just the education of the Indians. Just as important, and even more urgently needed, is the education of the non-Indians. Ignorance, bigotry, intolerance, sentimentality, discrimination, all have to be conquered before what is generally called "the Indian problem" can be solved. But is it an Indian problem?

When a child is ill, hungry, and dirty, you cannot expect to pat him on the back and tell him "Go get it, boy. The world is yours." That is, expect him to be motivated. Motivation must surely begin earlier. True, we cannot hope to do much for the adult Indian. However, if we furnish him with a climate of learning and thorough adult education, he may take enough pride in learning to inspire his children.

The problem, which faces my people socially, economically, and politically, is necessarily a cultural one. It is a challenge to civilization.

Today, almost all the citizens of Canada and the United States are aware that something must be done. By far the most encouraging and imaginative work done among my

192

people (not excluding the millions of dollars spent by both Canadian and United States' governments) is carried on quietly by the Mormon Church, the Church of Jesus Christ of Latter-Day Saints (LDS).

In conjunction with the seminary program conducted by the Church Department of Education, more than thirty-seven hundred Indian boys and girls were attending seminary classes and enjoying seminary-related activities as far back as 1963. Twenty-one professional teachers and more than one hundred fifty volunteer teachers are engaged in the direction of this work.

As early as the 1962-63 school year, Indian seminary classes were conducted for students who attend almost one hundred federal and public schools which extend all the way from the Mohawk community at Hogansburg, New York, to the federal schools at Riverside, California, and Salem, Oregon.

The Church Department of Education is developing a specialized Indian seminary curriculum suited to the needs of the Indian students. Heavy emphasis is placed upon providing opportunities for the students to develop talents and leadership qualities. Excellent facilities, including classrooms, chapel, and recreation area, have been provided in new seminary facilities adjacent to several of the larger off reservation boarding schools. Such buildings are presently in use at Albuquerque, New Mexico; Riverside, California; and Brigham City, Utah. Another is under construction in Stewart, Nevada; and other building sites are presently being sought at Phoenix, Arizona; Salem, Oregon; and at a number of additional locations in the southwest. A home was purchased in Lawrence, Kansas, near the Haskell Institute, to provide for the activities of a growing number of LDS students in that school. A building program is also under way at Pine Ridge, South Dakota.

At several of the schools, a large enrollment of LDS students has made it possible to organize Indian student

193

branches where the full round of church activities is provided. These organizations provide additional opportunities for our Indian boys and girls to develop qualities of leadership and responsibility. They also provide the understanding counsel and direction of branch leaders who have a special interest in the Indian youth.

The entire scope of the seminary program is designed to help the Indian young people become better acquainted with the principles of the gospel of Jesus Christ and to give them practical help in applying these principles to the way they live.

The student placement program provides reservation Indian children who are members of the church an opportunity to spend the school months in the homes of non-Indian LDS families while they attend public schools at the foster family location. This program is under the direction of the Relief Society organization of the church, which operates as a licensed social welfare agency in the state of Utah. The Arizona Relief Society holds a similar license for that state.

Eight professional case workers are employed by the church to look after the welfare of the students who enter this program. They also help the foster families to understand the background of the Indian students, and are instrumental in promoting wholesome adjustments, both for the students and for the families with whom they live.

The stated objective of the Indian student placement program is "to make possible educational, spiritual, social, and cultural opportunities for Latter-Day Saint Indian children, and to provide opportunity for them to participate in non-Indian community life so that they can use their experiences now and later for their own benefit and that of their people." This program exists primarily for the educational opportunities it affords the Indian children it serves. These opportunities consist not only of those experiences in the formal school situation, but of the informal training received in the home and the church.

194

Participants in the placement program are selected on the basis of recommendations of missionaries, teachers, or other church leaders who know them well. In order to qualify, the child must have permission from his parents, be a member of the LDS church, be in good physical condition, have adequate competency in the English language, and have demonstrated his ability to perform schoolwork appropriate to his age-grade level.

Each child is carefully interviewed by a caseworker, as are all of the foster parents. Every effort is made to place the children in homes where there is the greatest possibility for happy, wholesome living.

During the 1970-71 school year, there were 5,000 children representing fifty different tribes participating in this program. They are living with Latter-Day Saint families in Utah, Arizona, California, Oregon, Idaho, Washington, Georgia, South Dakota, Nevada, and North Dakota. This plan had 507 Indian children, representing fourteen tribes in the 1962-63 school year in only two states.

As far back as 1962 the Church of Jesus Christ of Latter-Day Saints operated a full-time Indian mission among the Indian people of the following states: Arizona, New Mexico, Wyoming, North Dakota, South Dakota, Minnesota, and parts of Colorado, Utah, Montana, and Nebraska. There were approximately ten thousand Indian members of the church within this mission. The mission headquarters are in Holbrook, Arizona.

Even as early as 1962 more than two hundred eighty missionaries were devoting their full time to serve the Indian people. They were filling mission terms of two years duration at their own expense.

Other Indian areas within the United States, Canada, Mexico, Central America, and South America are also served by other church missions, in which thousands of young men and women are devoting their full time to missionary work.

Throughout the Indian mission, members are organized

195

into wards or branches where they help to assume responsibility for the leadership and direction of the local church organizations. They are given opportunities for service and for developing their skills and talents. Many of the branch organizations have as their presiding officers Indian members of the priesthood.

The church also directs other missionary endeavors for the benefit of the Indian people. Stake and regional missions are organized throughout the church in areas that are not served by full-time missions. In these areas hundreds of dedicated men and women are engaged in missionary activity on a part-time or church service basis. Some of these organizations, which have a special orientation to the Indian needs, are the Uintah Basin Regional Mission, the Salt Lake Regional Mission, the Pocatello Regional Mission, and the Southern Pahute Indian Mission. There is also a regional mission in Ogden, Utah.

In metropolitan centers where numbers of Indian people are relocating to seek off reservation employment opportunities, the church has appointed specially-called Indian coordinators, whose duty it is to assist Indian members to make proper adjustments in their new surroundings. Such coordinators have been appointed on a church service basis, usually under the direction of stake presidencies, in each of the cities where the Indian Service operates Indian relocation centers. An effort is made to make the Indian families acquainted with other members of the church in their locality, and to make available to them all of the opportunities and services enjoyed by church members.

Even as far back as the summer of 1962, the Church Department of Education sponsored summer activity programs in two locations — one at Fort Washakie, Wyoming, and another at Albuquerque, New Mexico. These programs were carried on for the particular benefit of the youth; and upwards of two hundred fifty young people participated in the two locations. Activities ranged all the way from

196

organized recreation and competitive sports to photography clubs and music instruction. The Albuquerque group presented a television program and concluded their summer activities with an excursion to Carlsbad Caverns. Professional directors and their families were employed by the church to supervise these activities. It is hoped that new programs can be expanded to other Indian areas in the years to come.

In 1970 there were five hundred and twenty Indian students at the Brigham Young University (BYU). They represent most of the Indian tribes. Many of them are attending the school on special Indian student scholarships offered by the church university.

The BYU maintains an Indian Education Office and employs a qualified guidance staff for exclusive service to Indian students.

The Indian student social unit on the campus is known as "The Tribe of Many Feathers." They sponsor a variety of special activities which, last year, included the National Indian Youth Conference and the National Indian War Dance Contest. The latter event was held in the BYU field house before a capacity audience.

Recently the Institute of American Indian Studies was established as a part of the Brigham Young University and the Unified Church School system.

The institute serves as a research and service organization, making available the resources of the university for study in areas of Indian history and culture, as well as for offering more practical assistance in the area of current Indian problems.

One project of the institute in 1962 was the production of a film on alcoholism in cooperation with the Navajo tribe. This film was in the Navajo language as well as English.

By direction of the first presidency of the church, there operates among the general offices of the church, the Church

197

Indian Committee. All of the committee members have a deep interest in the Indian people, as well as a broad background of experience in Indian work.

As more programs became available for my people and as coordination between existing ones become more effective, the progress of my people toward a fuller participation in modern life will surely come to pass.

The So-Called "Indian Problem"

My people have never been left to run their own course, since the white man first came. When the first white man arrived to disturb our way of life, our ancestors should have known that things could never be the same again. It is easy to see, now, where the mistakes were made, where the faults lie. Nevertheless, today's society has inherited what the white man calls the "Indian problem." Most people like to think that it is up to the Indian to straighten it out. But there is another way of looking at it. Is it an Indian problem? Or is it "the white man's problem?"

If it is really a white man's problem, what is the problem? What started it in the first place? Perhaps it was avarice, or lust for power. History shows that the newcomers weren't content to trade in peace with the inhabitants they found here. They couldn't live side by side with the natives. They were invading in such numbers that they were bound to take over the country, stealing more and more of the Indians' birthright, spreading the diseases of greed and dishonor that seemed to be a part of their civilization. That is when the white man's problem began with profiteering, with double dealing, with suppressions and massacres, with petty tyrants sent to govern the newly colonized country, and with treaties. That is where it started, in untrustworthiness, bad manners, and the white man's contempt for the subject races. That is the white man's problem — the same problem generation after generation. It is still with us today, modified in keeping with modern "enlightenment," yet magnified by the years of building up — a legacy most of you would be ashamed of — if you would take the time to be aware of it. The thinking was twisted and the Indian was blamed. The white man says that Indians couldn't be trusted. As far as employing one, they couldn't instill confidence. They are shiftless, dirty, untrustworthy, they are not capable of punching a time clock. They haven't taken the trouble to learn how to fit into working communities. They are willing to stay on the reservations and just be lazy and self-indulgent. They contribute nothing to the community.

Very few white people really accept Indians. Indian centers are being formed to mix the whites with the Indians, for each to learn the other's ways and each other's cultures. Many white people in the city don't know how the Indians live on reservations. They still think we are wearing buckskin clothes and live in tepees.

It is the responsibility of Indian leaders that few non-Indians have the time or interest in Indian affairs. This is a white man and Indian leader problem. What do you know about this small portion of the population? Are they any different from the giant portion of the population? In actuality, Indians are very similar in the basic concepts to the rest of society.

200

If you meet a good man, he is a good man whether he is an Indian or white man. An Indian is just as good as any white man; he is a good husband and a good father. What is wrong with marrying an Indian? Is it the color? Is it public opinion? Or is it because an Indian finds it harder to get a job? Or the thought of maybe going back to the reservation without the comforts of city life?

The educated Indians, who are deeply involved in Indian affairs, find themselves equally accepted either in the Indian community or in the white community. It is interesting to note that the better educated people are, the greater their interest and understanding is in Indian affairs, and more readily do they accept my people as one of their own.

Many of the older generations of Indians, the diehards, are still very much opposed to intermarriage. They may be right. Integration may not be the answer. But the problem doesn't lie in whether or not white people marry Indians. It lies in the whole attitude towards the Indian — the suspicion, the contempt, the distaste, the discrimination.

We have already seen previously how difficult it can be for an Indian raised on the reservation, with poor education and little experience of life, to go out and work for a living; how difficult it is to get a job, to make friends, enjoy the basic privileges the majority of people take for granted. In too many cases, they were not allowed to go to a mixed public school until recently.

Some Indians are encouraged to relocate, but when they do the Indian Service cuts them off of Indian benefits. They encourage them to attend local schools, but they will not give them any grants. On the reservation, they can build a house through the assistance of the tribe, but in town that is different. They cannot get the lumber cheaply. That way, they have to pay for everything. So what happens? They build little shacks, with very low standards, lower than on the reservation. In town is where you find the worst habitation for the Indian. So it comes to the point that, because they have left the reservation, the government says, "We have no more responsibility for you." Local and state governments have not yet accepted this policy. So who is suffering? The Indian. In British Columbia, the people of the Nass River leave their villages to work at the fish canneries near Prince Rupert. And when the season is over, they are out of work. But the federal government has no responsibility for them once they have left the reservation. And the provincial government won't give them relief because Indians are a federal responsibility. So there is no relief, no work. They would do better if they stayed in the country, on the reservations.

Usually my people themselves will be the first to praise the efforts of the federal government. But inconsistencies like this tend to discourage them from making the effort to integrate with the non-Indian population, disillusion them, even make them bitter. Some of the white man's legislation has the same effect, though it was originally intended for the Indians' protection; such as liquor restrictions, for instance, imposed originally at the request of the chiefs at the time of the treaties. Only recently have the restrictions been relaxed and in Canada not yet in all the provinces. The Indian's real property — his house and land — cannot be seized for nonpayment of debts, so it is nearly impossible for him to take out a mortgage. Many businessmen, and many Indians themselves, are under the misapprehension that none of their property can be repossessed, so loans of any kind are often difficult to obtain.

My people can get a loan if it is just a small loan, say maybe four or five hundred dollars, like that but the banks can't seem to see their way clear for any big loans, because the Indians usually haven't any assets. My people can get credit. It just depends on the person. If he is a good man, he can get credit any place, whatever he wants. His credit is good. My people have always gotten along

202

with the white people, if they meet their payments. Whose fault is it that credit isn't explained to them properly? Perhaps the Indian superintendent in charge of the reservation could do more to help.

Drink is at the bottom of most of the trouble today among the Indians. They haven't learned to handle it. It is inconceivable that anybody can truly handle it. A great many white men, even with the length of time they have been trying to handle it, can't handle it today. The Indians seem to think that is part of the white man's life, so they try at first to be social drinkers. However, even among the so-called social drinkers, many become alcoholics. The government does little to reduce the drunkenness, which is a major problem with most Indians. In some towns where the local Indian population is large, the streets are littered with men and women and even children who try to drink more than they can hold.

Right now the Indian thinks that just because he has the right to drink, that he should drink all he can in one day. Alcohol is still a big problem. But legislation to stop the Indian drinking isn't any better than giving him complete freedom. It is easy enough for the white man to make laws. Telling other people what they can't do seems to be something the white man does best. But my people need something more than that. My people can help themselves to a certain extent, but the white man brought the liquor here, and my people look to him to do something about it.

Most people call it the Indians' alcohol problem. But isn't it really more of a white man problem? Certainly the rules and regulations seem to be almost instinctive nowadays. The whole history of Indian legislation is one of restriction. At some time or another, the Indian has been forbidden to do an astonishing number of things — forbidden to dance, to sing, to drink, to vote, to speak his own language, to pray to his own concept of God, to carve totem poles, to paint his face, to give away his possessions.

Some of these restrictions were brought about by the state, some by the churches. Presumably none were designed primarily to suppress the Indian, though experience has shown that this is what resulted.

They would have done better if they had asked the Indian, "What does it all mean?" They might have asked, for instance, "Do you believe in a God? They might have asked, "How do you arrive at this philosophy of giving and sharing?" They would have learned that my people did pray to the God. It was the God of all men. If the churches asked, the Indian would not have gone down so low prior to coming up again. The mission schools had a great influence on the government's suppressing the Indian. However, the authorities "meant well." And gradually the Indian is regaining freedom to do what he likes within the framework of normal law. He was given the federal vote. He is still, legally, different. What effect does this racial distinction have on the Indian citizens of tomorrow — youngsters who have already learned about the discrimination of the past? What effects have the past mistakes caused? Bounties on Indian scalps, Indians sold into slavery? Villages burned and crops destroyed? Whole groups, like the Baothuks, hunted for sport until they were exterminated? Thousands left to die of the diseases brought in by the settlers. Deliberate encouragement of heavy drinking to weaken the Indians' resistance to traders. Bootlegging, which still flourishes near many reservations. Perhaps the most serious mistake, which the Indian suffers most from today, is the white man's responsibility for the collapse of the Indian culture. Each group had its own social organization, its rules of conduct, its code of acceptable behavior, its religion. The white man made it clear that what the Indians had always believed in was mere superstition, not to be taken seriously. Having deprived the Indian of his own code, little was offered in its place. Certainly today the Indian is being encouraged to redevelop his old culture though most of the songs and dances that were part of the old ritual of living have been forgotten, and their revival is slow. Some control may still be necessary because such ceremonies as the sun dance and others were barbaric in the extreme. Great pain was inflicted, and young people were sometimes badly mutilated. These are all in the past, these mistakes. Let's return to the present. Are you any more enlightened now? Do you really know as much about the first American as you should? Do you behave towards them as you should? Are you even interested? And equally important, what is the feeling of the government?

In the non-Indian community, it has come as somewhat of a surprise to find how little the average citizen knows about the original inhabitants of this country. All citizens have a responsibility toward Indian citizens. However, it is quite apparent that interest is growing. More and more people are beginning to understand that they must try to improve the standards of living for the Indians, and also present opportunities for him to improve his own welfare. In so doing, however, let us avoid the paternalistic attitude which undoubtedly existed and which, in my opinion, did the Indian more harm than good.

Paternalism. This is the most modern of our mistakes. Doing too much for the Indian, making him dependent, destroying his initiative. Paternalism now, restriction a few years ago, repression, and persecution earlier; through the years these have been Canada's and the United States' reaction to "the Indian problem" — all part of the white man problem. Are you learning by experience? Will the Indian be able to take a fuller part in the society of the future? The picture is improving as you have seen. More improvements are on their way.

Perhaps you would be doing my people a greater and more enduring service if, along with the many services they receive, there was prepared a simple, matter-of-fact statement of the reasons underlying the nations' (Canada and the United States) ability and reason (other than the obvious treaty obligations) for making these services available to them; and that they (my people) will soon have to make do for themselves. A government to long endure must be of the people, by the people, and for the people. In the light of the events of the past hundred years, a government, too, must be of one people with support derived from all the people. This holds true for my people as well as the general population.

If my people do not want to live as they do, if they do not want to always be in destitution, always on the verge of starvation, they must come to realize that they, and they alone, can fully and adequately correct their circumstances. However, over two hundred million people stand ready to aid and guide and encourage them once they demonstrate that they are ready and willing to accept the full responsibilities of modern civilization.

A caution to the general population is in order here which can be learned from the Indian situation. Since government is moving ever further in the paternalistic direction, you must remember that no government can support its people, for the simple reason that a government must derive its support from the people.

Caution, also, to the fatalists who say that this is the direction taken by Europe. Isn't it true so goes Europe, so goes North America? This may be the direction that the past has taken. However, there is a startling difference between the past and the present and the future. The past cannot be changed. The present can be altered. The future is the fulfillment of societies' desires, conscious or otherwise.

Therefore, remember fatalists and remember well — no government can exist without the consent and economic support of the people.

A dramatic lesson, indeed, can be learned from the past two hundred years of government control over Indian

affairs. In every area of human endeavor, my people, who were the cared-for, possess substandard conditions. These conditions, it seems, the government is incapable of realizing. Therefore, if the government tells you "We will care for you," tell them "Thanks, but no thanks." That is unless you too want a life span of age forty-four and the other countless substandards which are peculiar to my people.

Integration: America Must Become One People

My people have been on a downward trail ever since the white man first came to upset our long-standing social organization. Our religion and our dances have been suppressed, much of our culture forgotten. The old way of life, the customs and traditions, the authority of the chiefs, the family discipline, all these have had to change as my people tried to adapt the white man's way. And my people didn't get much help from the white man. It is pretty difficult, changing your whole way of life in a few generations. But it could have been easier with the right kind of help. What my people did get was segregation, discrimination, poor education, the second best in everything. But there is

208

a new age beginning, and my people are looking forward to getting a fair chance in everything. Improvements have already begun, but there is a long way to go yet. Indeed a new day is dawning for the American Indian.

Discrimination and involuntary segregation are almost nonexistent, Indian children can get the same education as non-Indians. Now those looking to the future talk of integration — integration of my people into the non-Indian life, rather than continued isolation of all but the comparatively rare ones. How to achieve this integration is a matter of opinion. You will hear, "Close down the reservations and abolish the Indian services and make the Indians full citizens with full rights and responsibilities like the rest of us." You will hear, "Forget they are Indians and assimilate them like all the rest." You will hear, "Don't hurry the process; let them do it in their own time." Is any one suggestion the right one? Is integration such a desirable goal? Even the Indians themselves disagree on most points, but on one thing they are united.

Let us use the word integration rather than assimilation, because there is a great deal of difference. Integration means pride of your own racial characteristics, pride in your tradition, and the achievements of your race; but blending if you will with other people. Whereas assimilation is where the Indian as a racial or ethnic group would be completely merged and lost in the economy or citizenry.

Integration has to come. But we are not completely sold on the idea that once my people become white men, all of our troubles will be over. The white man seems to think he is being pretty big by letting us integrate, but my people have a lot of rights and privileges now that they may not want to give up.

Integration is going to come whether my people want it or not, or whether anyone wants it. This is a natural consequence of the fact that my people are a minority group.

209

It should be a natural integration, not an enforced one. Not one that is dictated by legislation which will breed bad blood. There have been policies in the United States where the government has tried to accelerate this program of integration and has caused considerable heartbreak and hardship in trying to do so. This should be avoided, and my people should be given every encouragement in the way of better education, better understanding on the part of the government, and of people generally, so that my people will quite naturally want to take a place in the community and want to become an active part of society.

Do you notice how education keeps cropping up? There is a pretty general feeling that integration must not be hurried.

It is a mistake, if we are just going to go in and lift my people off the reservation today and make white people out of them. You will never make a white man out of an Indian. You don't make a white man out of a Chinaman. You don't even try. He has to be a good Chinaman, the same with any other nationality. Therefore, an Indian is better being a good Indian than a poor white man. We are cutting the bridge behind them.

Yet, integration is going on all the time, faster and faster. Here again there is a difference of opinion. It is surprising. The Indian is integrating faster than you realize. Proper educational opportunities, the same as anybody else, are the solution. You must not forget that my people travel at their own speed, and some will lag behind. My people have been wards of the government for hundreds of years and they have not changed much.

Any program of education, or training, is only part of the answer. The white man needs education almost as badly as the Indian, only the white man's education should be in the facts of life. Educated Indians aren't going to get very far if the rest of the country doesn't want them, or discriminates against them, or looks down on them.

210

It is very hard for Indians to get good jobs. They still have that "lower class people look" according to the general population, and are looked down on as if they were the lower class. Look at my people as human beings. My people, on the other hand, must think that they are just as good as you are, and that they can do the same. If my people make mistakes, it is easy to fire them, but then you should look and see that they are just as human as you are. If you would only look at them as human beings, we would all be equal in this world.

My people don't advance with the times like white people. They don't have the experience in the field of agriculture and other areas of activity. They also have what you white people would call an inferiority complex. When talking to a white man, my people feel that if they make a mistake, you are going to laugh at them. Therefore, my people naturally come to accept the fact that they are government wards.

People in the city tend to judge an Indian by what they see in the lower part of town, the type of Indian that is constantly appearing in police court, the type of Indian that is drunk, who is looking for a handout. Any group will have this type of individual, and it is unfortunate that my people are judged by their undesirable element.

But my people are learning. And surprisingly the non-Indian is learning. It seems that the more they have to do with my people, the more sensibly they regard them. Acceptance of the Indian in the white man's community is almost as important as education. The education can fit them to take a place in the life outside the reservation, but as long as they feel unwanted, an undesirable situation will continue.

There are some who do go ahead. It creates a feeling of jealousy among the older ones, especially the ones who are trying to stick to their old ways of Indian life. This type of thinking does hold some young people back. This is what makes it difficult for a student who wants to go

211

ahead educationally. These students will go back home in some cases and the youngsters of the tribe will gather around these advanced students; they will mock them, they will tell them, "Oh they are trying to make a white girl out of you, they are showing you the white ways of doing things, they want to get rid of us Indians." They are going to mock them and ridicule them so much that most of the time the students will be discouraged and will not want to carry on. The enlightened Indians must go back and make them understand that this is not the aim. The enlightened white people do not want to make white people out of my people, but want them to become better Indians. The white people want to improve their lot. They want them to be capable of leading their own people so the Indians may be able to integrate fully, bringing in whatever they can to help society progress.

Mostly it is the old folks who try to stop the younger ones from going ahead. Perhaps in a few years this problem will solve itself. But still there are too many on the reservations who are living in the past, nursing grievances and refusing to face up to the changing times. There is a lot of blame pointing at the white man; but more of my people should be thinking positively, looking for ways to improve their conditions on reservations and their situation in modern society. Every Indian should think fifteen years ahead, or twenty years; because one of these days, the white man will say, "Well, we've been looking after these Indians for hundreds of years. If they can't look after themselves now, it is too bad for them." It is pretty well agreed that if an Indian needs help, give him help. But we have to get out and do these things. An Indian is just a man who is a victim of his own race. He is suffering for it now. It is your duty as members of the human race to help him and share his problems.

Education will give my people more footing. Each of my people must learn to pay his way. If my people start

212

doing that now, thinking ahead, then their children will be able to take care of themselves. Perhaps a little more of this kind of cooperation could help solve the white man's problem, too.

All of society seems to be becoming a race of mendicants. One of the first things they ask is "What is your pension plan? And what are your insurance privileges?" Forty or fifty years ago, it was a high privilege to have the opportunity of working. The government paternalism imposed upon the Indian has completely destroyed the initiative of a great many of them. If my people are to move ahead, they must quit living in the past and thinking of the misdeeds and injuries that were done to them and seize upon those opportunities that are presented to them now.

But here is a paradox. My people must stop living in the past, and yet they must not lose all those things which are part of their past — their language, their art, their music, their family pride. Every year fewer families use their native tongue. A few of the older folks refuse to learn English. Some speak English but prefer their own tongue.

The old dances are being revived in many areas. The government once suppressed them. Now the policy is to encourage them. So you'll often hear sounds like this coming from a man who may work beside you in the city. Back into the past — yet pride in their race and their culture is essential to my people's future. There are a great many aspects of Indian culture which could be very easily retained if the government and the white people had a better understanding of this culture, and understood some of the finer, better points of it. The two main problems are a lack of long range planning on the part of the government towards some intelligent end; that is, looking ahead to the time when my people will be becoming naturally integrated and not just planning for the day to day and the

213

year to year programs and expenditures. This has been one failing. Another has been the lack of personnel that are really trained in such fields as sociology, anthropology, etc., that would have a deeper understanding of my people's problems as they see them. The government, too, often sees the whole Indian problem, if it is to be called that, as an administrative problem and as purely a governmental white problem.

This is not an isolated criticism — though the government naturally doesn't agree. But what is the official aim of the government? What they are trying to achieve in Indian affairs is to help my people become fully participating members of the community. They should have the same rights, privileges and opportunities as their fellow man. My people must take on more responsibility for the management of their own affairs. This means transferring more authority to the tribes and helping Indians as individuals and as communities to do more for themselves. The Indians must develop a wholesome community life. They must be helped to improve their homes and community facilities and develop their resources. Progress depends largely upon education. By accelerating and broadening educational programs, Indian youth will be able to achieve the necessary training and skills that they need for successful adjustment into national life. Every opportunity must be given them to do so. The main task is to help my people become self-reliant members of the community with all the rights, privileges and responsibilities which are accepted and enjoyed by other citizens.

Education, integration, a different approach by both my people and non-Indians, encouragement of pride in race and culture; these are just some of the many suggestions for the future. But few of my people can achieve anything without the cooperation and the leadership of the government.

Only since 1924 have my people been considered citizens

214

in the United States. In Arizona and New Mexico, their right to vote was not confirmed in the courts until 1948. Indian youths have been drafted for military service only since World War II.

The events since 1924 have done much to make my people aware of the fact that they cannot alone decide the kind of future world they will inhabit. Furthermore, their experiences have shown them new ways of making their lives more secure and comfortable.

The proper role of the federal government is to help my people assume equal citizenship, maximum self-sufficiency, and full participation in American life. In discharging this role, it must seek to make available to Indians a greater range of alternatives which are compatible with the American system, and where necessary, to assist Indians with choosing from among these alternatives. As a part of this responsibility, it must mobilize and direct the vast reservoir of good will toward Indians which is found throughout the country.

So far as the future is concerned, there must come a day when my people will be entirely self-reliant, handling their own affairs like any other citizen in towns and villages across the Indian country. Over the past few years, there has been slow but gradual acceptance of responsibility by Indian leaders. The old idea that Indians are entirely the responsibility of the federal government should be gradually revised. The Indian leaders should be their own administrators to ultimately take the place of the governmental field staff. Naturally, this is a process which cannot be hurried. The conditions under which my people live vary widely. Accordingly, the degree to which they have already integrated is also far from uniform. The speed at which they will move is unpredictable. One thing is clear; the pace is theirs to set. There should be no pressuring nor forcing them. This would only create unnecessary hardship. My people will integrate into the social and economic life only as quickly as they themselves desire.

215

My people are halfway; they are standing on the horizon but whether they get all the way depends on their attitude and the help of the non-Indians, and on the policy of the government. This triple-edged sword must be held in the strong grip of understanding and swung surely by the strong arm of hope and desire.